This book is dedicated to Joe King
who was my friend once upon a time--

-

To: Diane

Purcell L Dixon

1

Joe King

C-130 PACAF

Joe King graduated from Memphis State University with a BBA in finance. He received his commission through the AFROTC program. Joe made the trip here from St. Paul, Minnesota with "Old Blue", the love of his life.

Joe is one of the classmates who is always "in the know." Like the time he said, "I heard some good poop in the John." Well, there must be something to it, because Joe once completely missed his takeoff and gave up his plane to someone else. Where was Joe? ASLEEP IN THE JOHN.

Joe recalls that his most memorable experience was his last contact ride in the T-37. He challenged Lt. Hoadly to a "High 6" aero duel which resulted in a change of flight suits before debriefing. Joe admits he lost the duel.

The Barfly decorates Barfly!

Prologue

This is a story about survival and the pain and suffering that is involved.

I thought about this story for years and years before I felt that I could begin writing it. It's not easy to revisit some of the things contained within.

I want my children and grandchildren to understand that we live in the best country on earth. You hear stories about how we are number seven on a list of all the countries in the world. Don't believe it. We are so far ahead of everyone else that they think they are in first place. We are in that position for two reasons: 1) Freedom and 2) resources. Some countries have freedom but no resources. Other countries have resources but no freedom to utilize them. We have both and are blessed for it.

In order to have them, we must protect them. We have tens of thousands of military personnel who go to extraordinary lengths to protect our freedoms. Some of those people come to life through this story, but it is not just for the military to protect our freedoms. It is the responsibility of everyone to protect them.

Ask yourself:

"What am I doing to protect my freedom?"

"Do I work? Do I support my family?"

"Do I support the military, police, firefighters?"

"Do I put my God and my country first?"

"Am I trying to be the best person I can be?"

If you can answer yes to these questions, then you are doing your part to protect our freedoms. If you read the story contained within and feel shame, then it is time to change the course of your life.

Russell Dixon

Table of Contents

Chapter 1 – School

I've always enjoyed school. That probably sounds like a contradiction coming from someone like me, but I couldn't find anything not to like about school. I remember most of my teachers because they all had some influence in molding my life and my personality. I can't remember all of their names, but their faces and personalities are fresh in my mind.

I especially remember my first teacher. She was the most special and influential of all my teachers. The lessons she taught me saved my life many times. She believed in teaching hard-headed boys the old fashioned way, by the school of hard knocks.

I was about five years old when I first met her. I lived on a dairy farm that my brother owned and operated. The farm was very remote with no other children close, so I had to amuse myself and invent my own play-world. All my brothers and sister were older and had left the farm, that is, all of them except my oldest brother who inherited and ran the farm. At this time, he had only been home from World War II about five years. When he arrived home from the war, Mama met him at the train station, and she was nine months pregnant. This came as quite a shock to him because he didn't know she was pregnant. Neither did he know that he would have to raise me. Nobody did at that time.

Chapter 2 – The Farm

Life was difficult in the years from 1945 to 1950, and it was especially difficult in the South because the South had not yet recovered from Reconstruction. The Civil War had been eighty years earlier and we were still struggling to provide basic needs such as food and shelter. The Depression had ruined the whole country during the 1930's and had pulled the South even lower socially. Then World War II came with all families being affected by that. Both my brother and my uncle had survived, and the whole family was rejoicing, but we were below poverty level and struggling mightily. We had a car, but it didn't run well, and we didn't have money for gas or repair parts. We mostly walked, if we could. We lived in an old farm house that my brother had built from nothing. He had piled up four piles of rocks for the foundation and built the floor on top of them. From there, he constructed five rooms and a roof. It was water-tight and it kept the wind out but modern conveniences were unheard. There was an old oil stove in the living room that provided heat; however, it only heated that one room. All the rest of the rooms were the same temperature as the outside.

We had an old electric range in the kitchen for cooking. This was our only modern appliance. It had replaced a wood burning cook stove. There was an ice box in the kitchen as well. The ice box was exactly that. It was a metal box with a door and a place to put a block of ice. This would keep food cool for a short time in moderate weather. The block of ice had to be replaced about once a week. If we didn't have the money to buy ice, which wasn't uncommon, you just stored your perishables in the cool shade of the spring.

Our house had no plumbing; consequently, the things that we take for granted today, such as water coming from a faucet in the kitchen and bath, were non-existent. Also non-existent were commodes, baths, and showers. There was no running water in our house. Each day someone would make a trip to the spring for water which we carried home in buckets. We used this water to drink, to cook with, for washing dishes, and for bathing. Needless to say, it was cold in the summer and frozen in the winter.

Electricity was scarce in our home as well. Each room had one electrical cord which hung from the ceiling. The range in the kitchen was straight-wired. There were no electrical outlets. Nothing could be plugged into an outlet in the wall. There would be one light bulb screwed into the socket in the cord hanging from the ceiling. The light was turned off and on with a little switch beside the socket. Invariably, the light would slowly swing in a pendulum motion, casting weird shadows around the room. The light bulbs were never over forty watts so each room was dimly lit and ghostly. That was always scary for a little guy.

The thing I remember most was sleeping through the night on a cold winter night. Only the living room was heated with all other rooms being closed off to conserve heat in the living room. That meant that bedrooms were the same temperature as the front yard. If it was twenty degrees outside, it was twenty degrees in your bedroom. We didn't have money for expensive comforters or warm bed clothing, but my Mama could make quilts from scraps of cloth. Any cloth that we could find would be saved to make a quilt. We used old flour sacks, discarded clothing, or anything else we could find or scrounge. When Mama had enough scraps, she would make a quilt, and it was highly prized. On a cold night, it would take a stack of ten quilts on top of you to keep you warm. You would have to duck your head under all that cover and make a little nest right in the middle of the bed. The initial dive under the cover would be so cold that it would take your breath away, but if you got your little nest formed and were absolutely still, you would begin to warm-up because of your body heat. It took about ten minutes of shivering and teeth chattering, but soon a warm radiance would settle over you and you would be as snug as a bug in a rug, provided you didn't move. If you made the mistake of moving anything, then cold air would flood your little nest and you have to start all over again building body heat. We all learned to sleep in one position all night without moving a finger. Also you had to become accustomed to the weight of ten quilts. One quilt would weigh about five pounds, so ten quilts piled on top of you weighed at least fifty pounds. That was more than I weighed and it took some effort for a little guy to get in and out of bed.

When your feet hit the floor in the morning, you were in for the shock of a lifetime. Standing naked, in the middle of a twenty degree room while you dressed, was a real bummer. As you walked barefoot across the floor, you left your footprints in the frost covering the floorboards. Getting dressed in the morning could have been an Olympic event timed in mere seconds.

Heaven help anyone forced to go to the bathroom in the middle of the night. That meant a trip to the outhouse which stood about fifty yards away from the house uphill following a small path. It was surrounded by a huge blackberry briar patch and was unheated and unlighted. Since we didn't own a flashlight, the whole thing had to be accomplished in Stygian darkness. That was spooky winter or summer. You could hear some really scary sounds outside the walls of the outhouse. If you didn't have to go too bad before you got there, you surely would after sitting on the hole for a minute or two. It could take five minutes to walk to the outhouse, but it only took five seconds to return to the house. When I grew up, I was always one of the fastest runners in any school I attended, and I attribute most of my training to those midnight mad dashes back to the house from the outhouse. It also taught me that the shortest distance between two objects was a straight line. I knew math before I even attended first grade.

Chapter 3 – Playtime

I lived in this old farm house for the first five years of my life, and I was a happy go-lucky little boy. Since we were so isolated, I had to play alone. There were no other children and I didn't have any toys. I had to use my imagination to devise games that I could play alone. A stick became a gun that I could shoot at bad guys. Rocks were prized because you could throw them at anything, including chickens and also the side of the house. A small stick could be a knife and could be carried in your back pocket. Another stick became a bat and walnuts lying about were balls that could be hit in the air and at objects close by, including chickens and the side of the house. The trees, outlined on the horizon were mountains, and I named each of them and learned to navigate using them as guides. Cloud formations formed horses, dogs, and guns and would then change to form mountains or houses. I would lie on my back and watch the clouds for hours and imagine what it would be like to be up there with them. I never knew that one day the cloud formations would be my home.

One thing I dearly loved was playing cowboy and Indians. Of course, I was the cowboy so I had to devise some kind of Indian. Being isolated as I was the Indian couldn't be another child and Mama didn't like me chasing the chickens because they wouldn't lay eggs for a week, which meant no breakfast. My solution was ingenious. The main road to town ran in front of our house and was about a hundred yards away across a field. It seemed logical to me that cars coming down the road could be considered an Indian on the warpath. Sometimes we could have as many as two cars a day come down that road. Everything I knew about Indians suggested that they were blood thirsty and you had to hide from them, so when a car appeared on the road in front of the house, I would run hide behind the first thing I came to that would offer protection from arrows. I would stay there until I had lost the blood thirsty Indian, then I would resume my regular play. Since I played cowboy and Indians a lot, I would use this same technique on every car traveling on our road.

It didn't take long before the busy bodies in town noticed my strange behavior and concluded that I was "slow" or perhaps mentally ill. Everyone knew that I never saw another child and on my infrequent trips to town I was very "stand-offish." Of course that was because I thought they were crazy, but I never verbalized my conclusions. They spread the rumor that I was "touched." These stories spread like wildfire around the Cotton Mill until some high-minded woman made the mistake of confronting my Mama about my "touched" condition suggesting that my Mama was unworthy to raise a child. As soon as the blood was cleaned-up and the ensuing dust cloud began to settle the rumors stopped. There was never another mention of me being "touched." My Mama had a reputation of being mean and tough and everyone knew it.

Chapter 4 – The County

One reason that I used cars for Indians was because of the dust trail that fanned out behind the cars. Anybody in their right mind knew that Indians left dust trails, and our road was an unpaved, dirt road. Actually, most of the roads in South Carolina were dirt at this time in history. Only the main State roads were paved. Not only were they dirt, they were a special kind of dirt—red clay. The clay in much of the Piedmont south is clay that is very high in Fe_2O_3 which gives it the characteristic red color. Usually jungle soils will leach over eons of time and form the red clay we have today, and has a mineralogical composition that forms into large thin sheets like notebook paper stacked together. Weathering causes these sheets to tear, much like you would tear a sheet of paper. Before the tear occurs, the sheets of clay are electrically neutral, but the tear exposes the electrons in the sheet. This causes the torn edges to become negatively charged, thus exposing small positive charges on the faces of the sheet. What was a perfectly neutral electrical balance now becomes a small microscopic magnet with the faces repulsing each other, the edges repulsing each other, but the edge to face exposures having high attractive values. Slowly over time, the edges stick to the faces and form a solid mass resembling a stacked card house when seen under intense magnification. The magnetic stacking forms a mass that is hard as rock, so dry red clay is very difficult to work with. It is difficult to plow and post-hole digging can cause a priest to turn protestant. However, if those bonds can be broken, red clay becomes a soft, malleable substance because the magnetic edges and faces have been moved apart and are no longer strongly attracted.

One way to move the bonds apart is water, which can flow into the interstices in the card-house and push them apart. What you have then is little flat sheets of clay rolling around on little ball bearing water molecules. Now you have something like a skateboard operating on very well-greased wheels that can go in any direction.

Picture the red clay dirt road in front of my house when the weather was dry. It would be hard as concrete and easy to drive on. The only problem is the dust cloud that forms behind the car. Now picture the road after an intense summer shower. It looks like the same road, but the card-house has absorbed the water and all the clay sheets have become mobile on little water ball bearings. Nothing happens until a force is applied and the sheets begin to scoot in all directions. You can't stand on it and you can't drive on it. A vehicle sitting completely still in the center of the road will gently slide into a ditch and will be stuck until the clay dries and the magnetic forces come back together. A summer shower will shut down all transportation on a red clay road system. It was always fun to sit on my front porch and watch cars attempting to navigate after a shower. Some of those farmers could really cuss.

Chapter 5 – Patsy

My life for the first five years was idyllic. I was completely happy although somewhat backward and quiet. I had nobody to talk to or play with, but I developed a very healthy imagination. Then my Father passed away and life began to change, slowly at first but as time went on, the progression from good to bad would accelerate.

My brother built a small two room house beside the farm house and he moved into it. My Mama moved away and my brother took on the responsibility of raising me. He was good to me so the transition was seamless, although losing a family was difficult for both of us, and we began another part of our lives. My brother began buying dairy cows and built a milking barn. We went right into the dairy business.

That was when I received my first introduction to my first, and most influential, teacher. I came to love her like no other in my life. She was rather short, about two feet tall, and she was black. In 1950 in the rural south being black and having the responsibility of nurturing a white child was uncommon, but she accepted the job anyway. She was kind and gentle with me but had the ability and aptitude toward harsh punishment if I got out of line. To make her job even more difficult, she was mute and could not speak a single word. It was entirely up to me to learn by example. You may think that this would be a huge impediment, but since I had never had anyone to talk to, this became a seamless adjustment. I did not think that her being mute was any problem whatsoever. We bonded instantly.

Did I forget to mention that she had four legs and floppy ears? She also had large brown eyes and a bushy tail. She was an English Shepherd and her coat was so shiny that it looked iridescent in the sun. I was in love. I named her Patsy, the prettiest name on earth.

My brother correctly surmised that I needed someone to play with, but he had an ulterior motive as well. He needed something to help him herd the cattle; therefore, he solved two problems with only one transaction, and my schooling began immediately.

Chapter 6 – The Barn

He had built a milking barn out of cement block, and it was located on a hill adjacent to the farm house some five hundred yards away. The barn only had two rooms. One was used to corral the dairy cows as we milked them, and the second room contained the milk cooler, which was a metal container holding salty water. The milk would be poured into metal jugs that were water-tight. These jugs would be immersed in the water, and the milk could be stored very close to freezing, keeping it fresh.

The milking room had metal stalls imbedded into the concrete with head locks to hold the cows and a feeding trough in front of the head locks. There were five milking stalls in the room, but we had about forty cows that had to be milked. That meant that we had to rotate five cows at a time into the room, get them into a stall, lock their heads in place, feed them, and milk them before rotating another five cows into place. Since the milking room was rather small, absolute order had to be maintained or you might get hurt or one of the cows might be hurt.

All forty cows would be herded into a corral adjacent to the end of the barn. A door opened at that end that would allow cows to enter the milking room. Once finished, a door was opened out the front of the milking room, and five milked cows would exit the milking room to spend the night grazing in the pastures which ranged far and wide across the farm.

You might think that a dairy cow is a stupid creature that could not learn anything and is incapable of being taught complex maneuvers such as these, but you would be very wrong. We wanted eight waves of five cows apiece to voluntarily come into the milking room and walk directly into their milking stall. We wanted the cows to remember which one of the eight waves they belonged to and to wait their turn until it was their wave's turn to be milked. We also wanted each cow to go into an assigned stall each day and not fight over the stalls. That meant that they had to be able to count to eight, to know the correct wave to get into, they had to count to five to know which stall to walk into, and they had to align themselves from one to five in a line before entering the milk room. The first cow went into the first stall with the second cow going into the second stall all the way to number five going into the last stall. We wanted them to arrive in that precise order every single day. When they were milked, we opened the front door and then opened all the head locks. The first cow walked out of the milking room while the other four held their places, then the second cow would exit until all five had exited in an orderly manner.

It took the cows one day to learn this. It took two milking's, one in the morning and one in the afternoon. Never think that a cow is stupid.

Never think that an English Shepherd is stupid either. Now we had a herd dog that had to learn this intricate bovine ballet. We were very nervous because herd dogs do not take guff from large cloven-hoofed animals. We did not know what kind of chaos she might bring to our orderly procession of milk cows. All we could think was to position her next to the doors and let her watch, which, we prayed she would do quietly. We didn't want a rodeo inside that small room. We got her positioned and opened the door for the first wave of five cows. They were very, very concerned about having to walk by this creature with long white teeth and flashing eyes. Quickly the first cow sidled by, rolling its eyes toward her as she jumped by and then the second and third went by with much temerity until we had all forty milked and out the door to pasture. Patsy never moved a muscle, but she did not miss a movement either. From that moment forward, she knew the exact sequence of events. She would lie by the door with nothing moving except her eyes as each cow passed; however, if one of the girls got uppity and tried to break in line, she would be out the door like a black streak with order being restored within a moment. It only took her one time at watching the milking process to have it all memorized. She was truly exceptional and expected me to be the same way.

Chapter 7 – Milk Day

Farm life was a lot of work and it was never ending. The cows had to be milked twice a day and milked every day. That made it a 365 day job with no week-ends, holidays, or vacations. We would rise at five a.m. each morning and eat a large country breakfast. Then we would head for the barn for the first milking. Usually the girls were hungry and ready to be fed and milked. If they were not milked on time, their udders would swell and it would be uncomfortable for them, so they were always waiting on us. We had to milk them, transfer the milk to containers which were placed in the cooler, and then the milking room had to be thoroughly cleaned. About twice a week the milk company would send a large truck to the barn and we would load the cooled milk aboard. It would be taken back and measured for fat content. You got paid more for higher fat content. They would cut us a check and return it to us. That check was our sole income.

It was a lot of work, and I was my brother's shadow. He was never able to go anywhere without me tagging along and I did any work that I was big enough to accomplish. I would open the door to the corral and bring in each wave of cows to be milked. I would then close the corral door and lock each cow into her stall. Then I got feed and gave each cow a measure of feed. I would open the exit door as my brother finished milking, and release each cow. Patsy would monitor their orderly exit. My least favorite job was shoveling any poo poo that might hit the floor.

When the milking container was full, I helped my brother transfer the milk to a storage container which would be stored in the cooler. This was a simple task of pouring milk from one container to another but it was a challenge beyond belief for my brother. World War II had not been kind to him. All the fighting had caused him to have a break down sometime during the war. He had to be hospitalized for a period of time in Hawaii and allowed time to recuperate. He recovered almost entirely, but not completely. He still had the shakes. His hands trembled substantially, and he had no control of it. As he attempted to pour the milk from one container to another, his shaking was so violent that the containers would rattle together and milk would spill. It was my job to be his steading force. I would help him stabilize the milk container so that it flowed properly. I was only six or seven years old at the time and did not understand the significance of that simple act. To me, his shakes were just a part of life to be accepted and adjusted for. He eventually recovered from the shakes, but it took another twenty years. He would struggle mightily with simple tasks like pouring gasoline into the tank on the tractor or lighting the fuse on a stick of dynamite. I wouldn't even consider being anywhere else rather than beside him steading his hand.

My Mama had three boys and she sent all of us to three different wars. We were spaced in age to be unlucky recipients of World War II, Korea, and Vietnam. We all came home with our hides intact, but our minds suffered the bullet holes of war. There was rejoicing when we returned but also a period of adjustment.

My Mama was Irish so we got the gift of storytelling from her. Both my brothers were wonderful oral story tellers and could keep you entertained for hours telling one story after another. However, I don't even remember hearing one single story from either of them regarding their respective wars. We all three walked away from these.

The morning milking took until noon. The barn would be clean and ready for the evening milking, so we would wander home and have a large dinner. In the South Lunch is called dinner and the evening meal was called supper. Dinner was a big deal to us. We would have been working hard since five a.m. and would be starving. We would have lots of fresh vegetables steaming hot, mashed potatoes, and home-made biscuits. All was chased down by a half gallon of fresh milk apiece. After that little snack, we would be ready to work in the fields. We grew our own feed for the cows which included hay, corn and sugar cane. All this was in addition to a big garden.

Chapter 8 – Afternoon Play

In the spring the fields had to be plowed and prepared for the crops, so we would plow from noon until three p.m. At three p.m. we would stop and herd the cows to the barn for the evening milking.

Patsy and I loved plowing. I was too little to help so she and I would play and wrestle in the plowed earth. The sun would be warm but not hot and the smell of the plowed earth was so invigorating, but the thing we loved most was the flying grass hoppers. They were big and brown and made a loud whirring noise when they flew. They could only fly about fifty feet before they had to land to rest. Patsy and I would have contests to see who could catch the most grass hoppers. I still swear that she could keep count and would be relentless until she caught one more than I did.

We would follow along behind the tractor and allow my brother time to scare one up. When a grass hopper got airborne, it was a race to see who could catch him. The rules were simple because there were no rules. Patsy didn't believe in being encumbered by a bunch of dumb rules, and she quickly taught me that she intended to play rough. Once a grass hopper flew, she would use any number of under-handed tactics to neutralize me. She would grab my britches leg and yank with all her might. That sent me face down in the plowed earth while she used my back to jump from in order to get a good head start. I would come up sputtering and spitting dirt and throwing dirt clods. My brother would just look at us and shake his head. O.K., so I was losing one to nothing. I knew that if I was to win this game, I had to use my head. Just running after a grass hopper was a useless form of offense.

The next time I saw a grass hopper fly, I slammed her in the side with my shoulder and sent her sprawling in a tangle of kicking feet. I couldn't stay and laugh at her because I was off and running. As I was reaching for the grass hopper, a black streak sailed over my head and her teeth snapped together like a bear trap inches from my fingertips. The grass hopper was history. She had jumped completely over my head and snagged the grass hopper while still airborne. I had not anticipated such athleticism and complete disregard for my fingertips. O.K., so it was two to nothing, that wasn't insurmountable. My brother just shook his head.

We got behind the tractor and began a quest for new prey. This time I pointed out something in the woods to hold her attention while I was off and running, and just in time for my brother had flushed another grass hopper. I knew I was way ahead of her this time and she couldn't jump over me. Just as I reached for the grass hopper, I was slammed in the back by a cannon ball. She had gotten up a full head of steam, made a long jump, and hit me in the center of the back with all four feet.

When I spit out that mouthful of dirt, she was sitting on her haunches with the dead grass hopper at her feet and looking at me like, "what took you so long?" My brother just shook his head. I was glad he was enjoying this because it was killing me. So it's three to nothing and not looking good. Actually, it looked like a shut-out unless I got better. We would have to stop plowing soon.

Patsy and I fell in behind the tractor waiting for another grass hopper. She had gotten wise to my tricks and was staying a good ten feet away so I couldn't grab her. My mind was racing. What could I do? She was a real handful with speed and athleticism her major attributes.

There he went, another grass hopper was on the wing like a quail in full flight, and we were both off. I tried to trip her, but she was too far away and her speed was unquenchable. I had to think of something or this game was a shut-out. Quickly, I took off my shirt and threw it at the grass hopper. It caught him in mid-flight and he went down with the shirt. This sneaky maneuver caught Patsy by surprise and she over ran the grass hopper, putting on brakes and coming to a sliding stop on her side. Meanwhile, I dove with all my might and landed on top of the shirt and the grass hopper just before Patsy arrived. Since I didn't actually have the grass hopper in my hand, I hadn't actually caught him. It was a technicality that Patsy grasped immediately. She began to dig dirt from underneath my stomach at an astounding rate. She was attempting to dig a hole and get underneath me, and she wasn't too concerned if she took hunks of my skin away with the dirt. Frantically, I put a hand underneath me from the opposite side and felt for the grass hopper. She already had her head underneath my stomach and was smelling for the grass hopper and rooting me in the ribs at the same time. That both hurt and tickled and was bringing tears to my eyes. Finally my fingers grasped the grass hopper and I rolled on my back and held the prize high. Patsy jumped across me, knocking the grass hopper from my hand and walked away disdainfully as if to say, "That didn't count because you cheated." It was three to one and I wasn't shut-out.

My brother had stopped the tractor and was standing over me looking down and shaking his head. He said, "Boy, that dog will make a competitor of you." "Come on, let's get the cows up."

Chapter 9 – Playful Instruction

The evening milking was a little different from the morning milking. One difference was that the cows had not had as much time to produce as much milk so milking time was shorter. If we let them go all night, they would produce too much milk and it would be very painful for them. The evening milking was just to keep them comfortable all night. Since their udders weren't completely full, they weren't as eager to be milked. In addition they had been continually grazing on grass and saw no need to stop. The pastures were a long way from the barn so they had to be herded across grass that they wanted to stop and eat. The sisterhood could be an erratic pain in the butt in the evening. That had been one reason why my brother brought Patsy to me. She was a herd dog, and she knew we wanted the herd to go to the barn. Sometimes the sisterhood would try to double back to the pasture and try to run by us. Sometimes they would run into any woods that we passed by and they would go round and round in the trees rather than head to the barn. All these slow- downs would prolong an already long day.

It didn't take Patsy long to show the sisterhood who was boss. She would keep them in a tight bunch all the way to the barn. She knew as well as we did that it was much nicer spending time at home rather than chasing cows through the woods.

We would finish milking about five p.m. and head home for supper. It would be a hot variation of dinner and was always delicious.

After supper, I would have a couple hours play time before dark. Patsy would be waiting on me. I saw it as play time but as I look back I now understand this afternoon time with Patsy was my time to be taught valuable lessons.

We played many imaginary games, but the two games we played most was fighting and playing ball. As with anything else, Patsy's games were simple. There were no rules and were meant to evolve as your skill levels progressed. The way we played at fighting today would be different by the next day. The main reason for that was that I had time to think about new things to try on her because the ones of the day before had failed.

Generally all I had to do to start a fight was to walk up to her and push her. She would use that as an invitation to attack me. She would grab my britches leg and pull me down. Then she would do everything in her power to pull my pants off. She knew I was a little shy and would hold onto them with one hand and that cut my offensive capabilities in half, giving her the advantage. The only way I could dislodge her was to put one foot under her nose and push. That cut off her breath and she would have to let go.

I would jerk my pants back up, but she would grab me from behind by my shirt collar. She knew just how to twist my collar so that it choked me. Just as I was getting tunnel vision, she would release the choke hold and use the slack to pinch me vigorously on the back. When she heard me inhale from the pain of those pinches, she would reapply the choke hold. She would alternate these miseries until the sun went down unless I found a way to break the choke hold.

I had to reach behind me with one arm and encircle her neck then kick her feet out from under her while rolling on top of her. If I could get a loud grunt with this maneuver, I could break the choke hold. She would then whirl onto her back with me on top of her. I would be struggling to control her legs. If I failed, she would push upward with all four legs, and I would go flying through the air to land on my back with a loud thump.

She would trot off looking over her shoulder with a smug look. Normally she would trot over and pick up our rubber ball and begin to trot in large circles. That was the signal to play ball.

Playing ball was nearly as rough as fighting. The main goal was to get the ball away from her and then throw it high in the air so that it landed on the roof of the house. It would bounce high in the air and arc back to the ground and became the object of a fierce fight to see who could reach the ball first. This sounds like grass hopper, but I had more of an advantage at ball. I didn't have to run as far and I was taller than she was. Now she had to overcome my natural advantages by tripping me, biting me, jumping over me, or using any other number of nefarious tricks.

The game was fun until she actually caught the ball, and she was very good at catching it. Then the game became a modified version of fight, with me having the advantage of her not being able to bite me. Of course, I had to catch her and that could be very frustrating. She would frustrate me every time she had an opportunity. She was teaching me to out think her.

Finally, it would get too dark to play and I would head for the front steps planning to go inside. She never made anything easy for me. She would let me get half way up the steps before grabbing the cuff on my pants and pulling me back down the steps. My chin would bounce on the steps as she yanked and pulled me to the ground. She would start pinching my leg and I would have to put my foot under her nose, break her hold on my pants leg and quickly scramble up the steps. Sometimes it would take me five or six tries before I could outrun her up the steps and into the house.

I would lie on the floor panting and sweating, totally exhausted. My sister-in-law would help me up, give me a cold glass of milk, and help me get ready for bed. It had been a long day. Every other day would be just like this one, seven days a week.

Chapter 10 – School Days

Bed time was special to me. My brother's house only had two rooms. One room was the living room and their bedroom combined. It had a television, two chairs and a bed. The second room was a kitchen and dining room. This room contained an oil heater which sat in one corner so there was a small area behind it. This area was just big enough for a small cot. That was my room. I didn't care if it was tiny. It was so warm and cozy behind that stove, and I didn't have to sleep with ten quilts on top of me.

I would sit at the table and drink my cold milk and then turn like a zombie towards my bed. It was only one or two steps away, and I would be asleep as soon as my head hit the pillow. On cold nights I could hear the fire from the coal oil burning warm and quiet beside me. There didn't seem to be a cozier place on earth.

My days clicked off one after another in happy harmony for the next two years. Then one day my brother came to me and said, "You've got to go to Grammar School tomorrow."

"Why?" "What's Grammar School?"

"That's where you will be taught reading, writing, and arithmetic,"

"Where is this place?"

"About ten miles up the road."

"I can't walk that far."

"You don't walk. They will come get you in the School Bus."

"What's a School Bus?"

"You will see tomorrow."

"Do I have to walk home?"

"No, you ride the School Bus home."

"Why can't you teach me?"

"I have to milk cows."

"I have to milk cows too."

"Not for the next twelve years you won't. You have to go to school, and then you go to college so that you can make something of yourself."

"Who says so?"

"It's the law, now go to bed."

That was the longest night of my life. I had no idea what school was, what teachers were, didn't ever remember seeing a book, and the thought of riding a school bus made my stomach churn. I had forgotten to ask if Patsy was going. I just assumed she would because she had been my constant companion and teacher.

I was quiet and withdrawn next morning at breakfast. Finally my brother said, "Come on." "I will walk you to the end of the driveway so you can catch the School Bus."

I said," How do you catch a school bus?" "I don't know anything about how to catch a School Bus."

"You don't catch it. You wait at the end of the driveway and it will stop for you to get on it."

"Oh." "Are there Policemen on it waiting to put me in jail?"

"No." "School is fun. You will see. I always liked school. I even wanted to be a teacher, but the war came along and changed everything."

The walk down the driveway was like the walk to the gallows. I really was backward and had not been exposed to anything but cows and fighting. Of course, Patsy was with me and sat beside me as I awaited the bus. Waiting for the devil himself would not have been more heart wrenching for me.

Finally the School Bus arrived in a cloud of dust, and I stood transfixed staring at this long yellow and black contraption that scared me even more. I wouldn't get on the bus alone. My brother had to walk me on the bus and get me seated.

I said, "You forgot Patsy."

"She can't go with you."

Immediately I was up and headed for the door. It took a lot of convincing before he talked me into a seat. He got off the bus and the doors closed. Patsy went berserk. The last I saw of them, he was on the ground with her and had a scissors hold around her middle and both hands on her collar. I don't know who had the worst day, me, my brother, or Patsy. I guess we all were a little backwards.

We arrived at the school house and the bus driver had to tell me to get off. I didn't know that this was the Grammar School. It just looked like an old brick building to me. My brother had graduated from High School here in the late 1930's, so the building was not a modern marvel. It was a two story structure with a hallway going from front to back and three rooms on each side of the hall. There was one extra room on the right side and I didn't know what it was. I figured it was some sort of torture chamber designed for backward farm boys. The kitchen and dining area was a completely separate building so the cooks wouldn't burn the school building down while cooking dinner, or lunch as they called it. They even called it the lunch room. It sounded crazy to me.

I wandered up and down the hall not having a clue as to what was going on. I thought, "Well, I've been to school, now it's time to go home." No such luck. A teacher finally concluded that I must be that slightly "touched" farm boy and gently guided me into my first grade classroom. About twenty sets of eyes were looking at me with a look of apprehension that must have been showing in my eyes as well. I would soon learn that we were all in this together suffering the same.

Chapter 11 – Classmates

This was 1952 and the building had been built about 1930. There were few modern conveniences. Each room had large windows that opened to the outside. If the weather was hot we opened the windows. That would be your air conditioning. There was an old stove in the back that gave off some heat in the winter. We all knew to dress warm if it was cold although not all of us were able to do that. In my day the special needs children sat right in the classroom with us. Usually they came from very poor families and they came to school year-round in tattered rags and bare footed. The rest of us were lucky. We got one pair of shoes each year to wear to school. As soon as the weather got warm, the shoes came off and we all went bare footed. My feet were so tough that I could run through briars and not feel a thing. We came to school bare footed until the weather was just too cold to stand the cold, then we would transition to wearing shoes. You would have to learn to walk again once you first put on shoes. The shoes made you awkward and clumsy and you would fall around.

We accepted the special needs children as part of our group. We never thought anything of it and we never made fun of them. Making fun of people is a bad habit that is taught to kids by adults just as racism and hatred are adult taught acts. Young children don't have that in them.

We allowed them to play in our games of Red Rover and Tag. We didn't care if they couldn't do them well.

Our classroom had high ceilings which made it much cooler in summer but more difficult to heat in winter. There was a partition in the back of the room with hooks on the far side. This was the Cloak Room, and we all hung our one coat on one of the hooks each day in winter. Before being allowed outside, we had to file back and get our coats out of the Cloak Room. Everybody in our class did that except for Johnny. He was our special needs child, and he didn't own a coat. He was always bare-footed and bare-headed. We would take turns letting him wear one of our coats at recess. They didn't always fit because he was a big boy, but we could read the gratitude in his eyes when he was allowed to be warm occasionally. Today, I go around school yards and see coats just thrown on the ground and forgotten. None of us would have ever done that. We only got one coat, and we knew what it was like to be really cold. Anybody from my generation would consider a coat thrown aside and forgotten as a sacrilege, a symbol of a generation without privation and respect for the treasures they own.

Class began once the teacher got me seated and informed me that this was my seat. I was amazed. I had never owned a seat before and this was a pretty good one. It had a little groove in the top for a pencil and the top opened up so you could store your treasures. I was beginning to like school.

As I looked around I was amazed at all the pretty girls, and they were all in my room. I remembered my brother saying that they had to be there because it was the law. I decided right then and there that we had some really smart lawmakers and that I would stay in school as long as I could.

I especially liked the little blue eyed one with the pig tails sitting next to me. I would soon learn that she liked to play cowboy. I was in heaven.

The teacher began to explain what we would learn and handed out a book. The book had pictures in it of a little boy and girl running around and it also had a bunch of scribbling. I just took her at her word. It sure looked hard to me.

About that time a bell rang and it nearly scared me to death. I thought somebody had died and the good Lord was coming down to recoup his body. The teacher said that the bell was for recess and we could go out and play. That was a relief. School was bad enough for my nerves and I didn't need to face the Lord that day.

The school yard was spacious and didn't have a blade of grass growing on it. There were large oak trees around which afforded shade in summer and large piles of leaves to run through in the fall. I guess that gave the school its name of Oakley Hall. I wanted to play and meet some of the other kids, but I had to pee really badly. I walked around the school looking for the outhouse but couldn't find it anywhere. I was getting desperate and I began to eye a large oak tree with increased interest. A teacher must have read my mind because she asked if I had to go, and then asked one of the older boys to take me to the bathroom.

I said, "Ma'am, I took a bath last week. What I got to do is pee."

The older boy grabbed me by the collar and yanked me into the school, down the hall, and into the room that I thought was a torture chamber. I forgot all about having to pee and my eyes got as big as saucers as I looked around.

I said, "What's this place?"

He said, "It's the bathroom." "Go pee over there."

I said, "What is that thing?"

"It's a urinal."

"Looks like a big white feed- trough to me."

"Just pee in it." "I don't have time to wait on you."

"What's that other thing?"

"That's a commode." "You do number two in there and then push this handle down when you are through."

I said, "You got to go on because I can't wait no longer." I was a little modest. He went stomping and muttering back out the door. Relief flooded my soul and I watched in awe as a little yellow stream ran down the white feed trough and disappeared down a hole. The marvels of science and school were all coming together for me.

I ran back outside and joined in the play. By this point in my life I had already had several years or working from daylight to dark, running, and fighting with Patsy. I could run across one hundred acres of plowed fields, meadows, and wood lands and fight like a ninja until dark. Patsy had molded me into quite an athlete which really helped me. I was terribly shy, but when the games started, I was better than all the rest. This allowed me to gain social standing and break through my radical quietness, although I've found that it never completely leaves you. I am still happy spending quiet time alone and am uncomfortable in a crowd.

Chapter 12 – Life Changes

Finally the school day ended and it was time to go home. This was an easy process for all the students except me and Johnny. There was a long line of School Buses and I had no idea which one to board. All the other students were lined-up for their buses. Johnny and I were standing to one side completely dumb-founded. The same teacher that saw me gazing upon the oak tree rescued me and put me in the proper line. As it turned out, Johnny and I rode the same bus so I was able to help him after this first day of trauma.

The bus stopped at my driveway, and I was off with a whoop and a bound. I had survived. Patsy was sitting on her haunches at the end of the driveway waiting for me. She flew into my arms and we rolled in the dirt with me laughing and with her whining and licking my face. My brother had not been able to make her move from that spot. She had sat there all day waiting for me. After she learned that I would return home, she would go back and stay with my brother until it was time for the School Bus to bring me home. At that time she would leave my brother and return to the end of the driveway and wait for me. She was always sitting there when I arrived and it didn't matter if it were raining, sleeting, or snowing. She would always be there for me.

That night at supper my brother asked what I learned in school. I told him all about the pretty girls and that you could pee inside the school where it was warm. He just shook his head. I knew he had hope for me, but he also knew this would be a work in progress.

Life would be idyllic for the next three years. My days were filled with school and learning and I seemed to be good at it. It all came easy to me and my mind was eager to acquire new skills. I got home in time to help my brother with the afternoon milking. Summers were filled with the same enjoyment I had before school had started for me and Patsy continued to teach me the art of thinking under stress. I was as happy as anyone could be. Then it all came crashing down.

I had noticed that my brother and sister-in-law had been having disagreements over whether we should continue with the farm or move to town. My brother was the farmer. It was his life but my sister-in-law wanted the luxuries that urban life afforded. Peaceful co-existence finally ended and they decided to divorce. That meant that the family farm had to go. It had to be sold with the assets being split between the two of them and all four had to go our separate ways. I still remember that as being the most tragic time of my life. I stood and watched as everything was auctioned off to strange farmers eager for a bargain. All had to go, the barn, the equipment, the tractor, all the cows, the houses, and the beautiful land with the meadows and streams. It was all gone in a matter of four hours, and I had to come to grips with the fact that I had no parents and no home. It was even worse for my brother for he had lost a wife that he never stopped loving. It was cruel. I couldn't wrap my mind around the pain. I was losing all this plus I would also lose Patsy. She went on to have a long life of loving children and teaching them valuable lessons. I am convinced that there is a doggie heaven and that Patsy commands a front row seat. She will be sitting there on her haunches awaiting me just as she waited for the School Bus each day.

Chapter 13 – On My Own

My brother could no longer take care of me. He was now broken in finances and in spirit. We had both lost a parent and a home for the second time. He went his way and I went mine. I was ten years old and by the time I was eighteen I had lived in twenty one different homes. I was never anywhere long before I had to go somewhere else. People were kind and tried their best to help me but times were tough and most couldn't help for longer than six months. I changed addresses routinely. The only constant thing in my life was school. I always applied myself and tried my best even though I didn't feel like it at times. I was good at sports and lettered on the varsity all four years of high school. My senior year I was voted captain of the baseball team by my team mates. I never talked of my circumstances but they found out. They all came from very well-off families and felt that gesture was the best thing they could do for me. They were correct because I have always been proud of that.

School gave me education, it gave me sports, it gave me structure, it gave me a home during the day, it fed me, and now it was about over. I had no intentions of giving up that easily. I had been accepted to both Clemson and the University of South Carolina. There was only one small problem. I was basically homeless and penny-less. Homeless I could deal with but college took major dollars and I didn't have more than forty dollars. I fell back onto a lesson Patsy had taught me—play sneaky.

I had heard that Springs Mills would sometimes give out loans to go to college for parents who worked for them and had a child accepted into a college. Well one of my parents was deceased and the other hadn't worked in fifteen years, but I didn't let that deter me. I took my forty dollars and bought a cheap suit and tie and a new pair of wing-tip shoes. I called Springs Mills and asked for an appointment to talk to the dude in charge of college loans. I told them my name was Mr. Dixon. They must have thought that I was somebody important because they scheduled me for ten o'clock the next morning.

I ironed my new suit and shined my new shoes and arrived at the appointed time. I walked in and shook hands with him and told him I was there for a student loan. He looked at me like I was someone out of the cast of Homer and Jethro. He only talked with employees who were applying for their child. I could see in his eyes that he didn't even know how I got in the front door. He stood there silently looking me in the eye for the longest time. There was no way that I was going to break eye contact because I knew my future started right there. At long last he sat and offered me a seat. Round one was over and I hadn't been thrown out on my ear. He was not used to dealing directly with the student and I could see him struggling with whether he should even try. Something prompted him to ask me one question, "does either of your parents work for Springs Mills?" I gave him my best level-eyed, cold-blooded lie, "yes they do and my brother as well." "You may know him, Donald Dixon." It was true that my brother worked for Springs but neither parent had ever been employed by Springs, and the contract stipulated that the parent had to be the one employed.

Don Dixon was my other brother and was rather well known and liked at Springs, and it is my guess that this guy knew

43

him and also the truth of my hoax. He just steepled his fingers and looked at them for a long time without saying a word. Finally he seemed to reach some decision that he figured he could live with. Probably he was figuring how he could under-hand this whole deal and not get caught. He dug a large stack of papers out of a drawer and handed them to me. He said, "Normally I fill out all this, but in this case I'm going to let you do it." "Whenever it asks for parent's name, just put Donald's name in there." That was one way of saying that he filed no fraudulent paperwork. I had no qualms at all. This was the beginning of the next phase of my life. That loan got me through Clemson and I made sure that I paid every penny back on time. That loan officer is sitting in heaven somewhere and Patsy licks his face every day.

Chapter 14 – Clemson

Once enrolled in Clemson, I noticed a big difference in teachers. High School teachers were concerned, helpful, dedicated to teaching and improving young minds. College teachers, or Professors as they preferred, were withdrawn and completely unconcerned about you, your study habits, or anything else about you. They simply didn't care if you learned or did not learn from them. They were withdrawn and heartless. Many of them had never had a single course in the art of teaching and were horrible at it. Some of them couldn't speak English well and didn't care if you could understand them. Most were totally dedicated to research and teaching just seemed to be something that got in their way. This is not to say that they were not smart. Generally, they knew more about their field of study than anyone else, and they would not hesitate to make you look foolish if you were the least bit unprepared for class that day. It was not that they cared if you learned, they just enjoyed being intellectually superior to those around them and students presented an excellent target for their egos. Many of them had written books on the subjects they taught and their books would be required of each student in their class. Many times the books were well over a hundred dollars and provided a nice income stream for them.

These Professors didn't care if you came to class or lay in bed all day. What happened to you was your concern, not theirs. The more people they forced out of their class, the easier it was for them. They had fewer people to teach and fewer papers to grade. Some of them were so mean that they had to grade on the curve or everyone in the class would fail. You could have a fifty average in some classes and still end-up with a B. This worked for Professors without tenure, for if they failed everyone, they could be fired. Once they achieved tenure, they couldn't be fired for anything, and it didn't matter if they failed all the students in their class. You learned who these crazies were and avoided them like the plague.

A lot of the guys at Clemson had a difficult time adjusting to the cavalier attitude of the Professors. They just couldn't get it through their heads that anyone would be allowed to treat them in such a brazen and callous manner. I had come up the hard way. To me, Clemson was heaven. It was home. It was safe. I had a nice room with a comfortable bed and a desk. The rooms had heat which was a luxury to me. You got three home cooked meals each day, seven days a week. I had never lived in such luxury. I gained forty pounds my first three months at Clemson. I no longer looked like a scarecrow.

Dealing with the Professors was just a game to me. I realized they were just making independent thinkers of these guys. It didn't bother me too much for I had been basically on my own since I turned fifteen. Living hard and having to calculate all the angles in order to survive was second nature to me.

The thing that bothered me was not the Professors so much as my grades. It was important that I make good grades. The loan I had would cover four years of school so long as I did not fail a subject. If I failed one course, it would be cancelled. I had no support outside of school. My only hope for a decent life was a diploma from Clemson, and I meant to get it.

The Vietnam War was raging at its peak, and there was a draft. If you were over eighteen years old, you had to register for the draft. If drafted, you would be toting a gun in Vietnam within three months. About the only exception to this were college students. If you were actively enrolled, you were exempt. If you dropped out of college for any reason, you would be drafted within three months. It was like death or taxes; you just couldn't get away from it. Once you finished college and got a degree, you were eligible to be drafted then. Some kids had parents with deep pockets, and they just became permanent students, going to school for years.

That never entered my mind, but Vietnam haunted me because I couldn't drop out for a semester and work to get money. If I did that I would be drafted and would never get back to school. I was constantly on the horns of a dilemma. My grades had to be good, and I was constantly penniless.

I learned to play the angles. I researched any Professor I may have to study under. If he had tenure and was a jerk, I researched ways to avoid him. Perhaps I could take that course in summer school when he didn't teach.

I found the old test pipeline. Students kept old tests and would sell them on the black market. A Professor can't ask but so many questions on a subject, and if you have three or four old quizzes on the subject, you stand a better chance of a good grade. Afterwards, you can sell the old tests the next year. The biggest dealers in old tests were the Frats. They had filing cabinets full of old tests on all Professors. I got in with the Black Market quick.

We organized study groups and compared notes. We quizzed anyone who had had the class before us. The Professors could play nasty, but we could play nasty too. It was a game of cat-and-mouse and the longer you hung with it, the better you got at it. Practice honed our skills.

There was one ray of sunshine about Professors that I noted. The Military teachers were different, remarkably different. In fact, they didn't call themselves Professors at all. They were Instructors. As I learned more and more about the Military, I noticed that the names that they gave things meant just exactly what it said. Instructors were just exactly that. They knew everything about a subject and they beat it at you, sometimes brutally, until you realized it needed to be learned.

Chapter 15 – Military School

When I went to Clemson, it was mandatory that everyone take two years of Military Science. If you took Military Science all four years, not only would you earn a commission as an officer, but you got a second major degree from Clemson and you got a monthly check from Uncle Sam for the last two years of college. This last scenario would prove to be a lifesaver for me. It was a way to get money just by going to school. What a novel concept. Why haven't civilian companies thought of this? If you want a dedicated employee, pay him to go to school and expect a commitment at the end. The results work surprisingly well.

Besides, I liked the Military and their Instructors. They stuck to the basics, just what you needed to know and they applied redundancy to be sure you retained it. They would ask you something seven different times during a study session. It might be asked seven different ways, but always led to the same answer. After seven times, your brain retains it. You don't have to go back to your dorm room and cram useless information. You already have what you need in your brain when you leave class. This principle of teaching remained consistent throughout my career and I found myself using it on my students. After the concept was in your head, you practiced it in real world conditions that were controlled but sometimes scary. If you passed this test, you were probably ready to face some really tough obstacles.

Professors were in the business of developing independent thinkers. The Military was in the business of developing men. The concepts were totally out of phase with each other. The

Military wants everyone to be able to work together and cover for one another. People can rotate in and out of a Military unit without any change being noticed by the unit as a whole. You only survive if everyone survives. If there is one person out of step then everyone is affected, hurt, or killed. It is all for one and one for all and this doctrine never waivers. If you receive some kind of training by an Instructor, everyone receives the same training. There are no people outside the system. Everyone knows what everyone else is doing, and they will be doing it precisely as they should.

In the civilian world, you are always a loner. Everyone else, even people on your own team, want your job and may be undermining the team effort. You have to constantly plot their work ethic to try to find any compromising situations. Everything is fluid and never stable, always in a state of flux. You have no friends on your right and left that you can depend on. Friendships are transitory and depend on your success at pulling others along. Training can be non-existent and expensive. Any time you are away from your job is an opportunity for disaster because people don't cover for you. Camaraderie is low and people have low self-esteem. The only measure of success is money earned. Day to day success where people work together is not even recognized. Things get done through fear of reprisal rather than any other reason. This is why the change from a Military environment to a civilian environment is so difficult. They are nothing alike. I did well in the civilian environment and had a successful career, but I flourished in the Military. They took a farm boy that was poor as dirt and afraid of heights and turned him into a jet pilot in one year, and it wasn't just me. All the guys in my Pilot Training class flourished and grew as men. By the time we pinned our wings on our chests we had the ability to be trained to fly any plane and deliver any weapon system with deadly accuracy. We were potential killing machines, proud, cocky, and brave. We had already scared ourselves to death and had survived and thrived.

The Military has two main missions. The first is to kill people. That was difficult to reconcile, but that was our mission. We had been trained, and we knew what we were doing. The second part of being in the Military was to keep from being killed. We had learned the first part, and now it was time to learn the second part. This is the beginning of the story I'm about to tell you. It's a story mainly of survival, but also courage and fear, co-companions of survival. It's a story about two old country boys from the South being thrown together in an environment like nothing either had seen before and living to tell about it. They learned a lot about themselves and a lot about how not to be killed.

Chapter 16 – New Orders

Pilot Training was over. I had been assigned to C-141's in Charleston, South Carolina. It seemed like a world away from Laredo, Texas where I had been in Pilot Training for a year.

Laredo had two seasons. In the winter, it was hot and dry. In the summer, it was even hotter and drier. It had rained two times in the year I was there. Both rainstorms had been scary enough to make you want to move away permanently. They had produced hail the size of baseballs and plenty of it. I have no idea how wild animals survived those storms. Both times the storms occurred at night when I was home. The hail beat on the roof so hard that you had to get beside another person's ear and yell very loud in order to be heard. When the storms were over, I went outside and the walls of my house were completely covered with mud from the hailstones burying themselves in the ground.

This was desert, but there were lots of wildlife. If you walked into the desert and stood quietly, you would see jackrabbits, small mammals of different varieties, snakes, lizards, birds, and bugs. The chaparral would be active with life. What was missing was water. You had to learn how to find it and how to conserve it, but water was here if you knew where to look.

I must admit that I never got used to the constant heat, even at night. When I got my orders, I was ready to leave and begin a new phase of my life.

I knew that I would be going to the Air Force Survival School in Fairchild, Washington. In my mind I envisioned a couple of weeks listening to lecturers and learning to tie knots and then I would be on my way to Altus, Oklahoma to learn to fly C-141's. I was excited about the C-141 assignment. It meant that I would travel all over the world and be able to experience sights and sounds from all parts of the globe. It also meant being stationed in Charleston, South Carolina. I considered all this as a major positive event, but, first I had to learn to tie knots.

I should have never been so naïve. I knew that the Military always called a spade by its correct name. You knew what to expect by the names attached to things. When I got my orders, they said I was to attend the USAF Survival Evasion Resistance Escape (SERE) School in Fairchild, Washington, and I should report by the middle of October 1970. There was a lot of information there and it should have given me pause. The word 'survival' means to continue to live after or in spite of some terrible event. The word 'evade' means to avoid or escape from by deceit or cleverness such as eluding a pursuer or to avoid answering directly any question. That should have told me that I would be chased for scores of miles, captured, beaten, and bullied, but it just went right over my head.

The word 'resistance' has several meanings, but it has one meaning totally dedicated to the military. It means it is the organized underground movement of fighting against a foreign occupying power. This school was beginning to take on layers of education that I had never had before.

The word 'escape' implies a getting out of, a keeping away from, or simply remaining unaffected by an impending danger, evil, or confinement. It is slightly different from evade which means to use artifice, cunning, and adroitness to avoid pursuit.

If I had taken the time to use my dictionary, my stomach would have had butterflies for a month. Years later, I researched this school by reading a little blurb that the Air Force publishes. It states the following: "Combat Survival Training is established to provide aircrews and other designated personnel procedures and techniques in the use of equipment and employment of survival principles. Graduates of the U.S. Air Force Survival School at Fairchild Air Force Base in Washington internalize the Survival, Evasion, Resistance, and Escape motto "Return with Honor." They spend weeks learning how to survive outdoors under any circumstances and to come home honorably."

"The majority of trainees at the USAF SERE School are Air Force crew members – pilots, navigators, flight engineers, loadmasters, boom operators, gunners, and other crew positions. Additionally, some intelligence officers and life support technicians may also attend. The school was created during the Vietnam War to prepare Air Force crews that were flying combat missions over Vietnam. As captured American air crews became Prisoners of War (POW's), the school was created to provide crews the skills needed to survive and potentially escape enemy capture in North Vietnam. Each course takes 19 days to complete. Students spend six days in the Colville and Kaniksku National Forests mountains, while the rest of the course is conducted at Fairchild. Students first learn how to handle the psychological and physical stress of survival, after which they learn post ejection procedures and how to handle parachute landings. They are also instructed in survival medicine. Shelter construction, gathering, cooking food, land navigation methods, evasion, camouflage, signaling, and aircraft vectoring are all taught during the student's six-day stay in the mountains. Before the trip to the mountains, they learn about how to behave if they are captured."

"You won't find too much concrete information or gouge on what to expect at SERE. This is designed so that the trainee can actually benefit from the training. The school is designed to be as realistic as possible and part of the realism is based on surprise and unpredictable stress you will experience."

"What you can do is make sure you are in shape. You will be hiking many miles a day with a heavy pack on your back while trying to evade capture – so make sure you are ready to do that. Make sure your gear is fitted properly and your boots are broken-in prior to the first day in the bush. Pack plenty of good quality wool socks."

That was a high quality understatement of facts. This school was going to be the most difficult school I would ever attend, one that would be hard-wired into my brain for years to come.

Chapter 17 – Travel to Fairchild

After packing my household goods from the little duplex in Laredo, I took my wife to San Antonio to catch a flight to Charleston. A friend from Laredo, John Ryan, had orders to Survival School as well so we made the plan to drive in tandem to Altus, Oklahoma from San Antonio. I would drop my car at Altus and ride with him to Denver. Once in Denver, we would store his car and both of us would catch a commercial hop to Fairchild. Once the Survival School was over, we would head in two different directions and not see each other again for years. That was the way of the military.

When we arrived in Altus, the weather was already noticeably colder than it had been in Laredo. John and I discussed this fact with much trepidation because we would be going all the way to the Canadian border. We were a little nervous at how cold it might be there. We knew we would probably spend some time in the mountains, and altitude would also impact the temperature significantly.

The trip to Denver from Altus was beautiful. The closer we got to Colorado the more splendid the scenery became. We began skirting the Rocky Mountains and the views were beautiful. The trip was uneventful except for the bar room brawl that John got involved in through no fault of his own. That happened in Pueblo, Colorado one night just after dark. John and I both had to run out of the bar with broken beer bottles slashing at John's hind-end on his way out. For some reason he thought he could negotiate a peace treaty between two Mexicans. Of course, John could only speak about seven words in Spanish and I think his pronunciation was so terrible that he must have insulted both of them. You see, John hailed from New Jersey and his thick accent took some getting used to, even if he were speaking English. Anyway, the Mexicans didn't want peace and they certainly did not want a peace negotiator. I hit the front door running full speed and John was only one step behind me. The problem was that the two Mexicans were only one step behind him and both were slashing with broken beer bottles. John was speaking seven words of Spanish over and over again and still managing to stay ahead of the two assailants. It was a truly impressive display of courage sugar-coated with a healthy dose of cowardice.

Finally the two Mexicans decided they hated each other more than they hated John, and we were able to make an escape. We didn't even get one drink of our beer. I said, "Dang, John, next time order your beer in a can. They can't cut you with that."

Chapter 18 – Survival School Classroom

We made it to Denver without any other mishaps and the flight to Fairchild was uneventful. When we bounced out of the airport, the air had a decided crispness to it. To me, the air was cold. John seemed to hold up to it better than I did. I had never experienced a bite to the temperature quite like this. We got rooms in the Visiting Officer Quarters and prepared to begin school early the next day.

The classroom part of the school lasted for about a week. The Instructors were knowledgeable guys who could live in the wilderness for weeks, and they worked hard to pass that knowledge along to us. Knot-tying was part of it, but we were shown a lot of stuff about preparing shelters, and staying out of the elements when inactive.. This course assumed that you had gone down somewhere hostile with only very minimal gear such as the clothes on your back, perhaps a parachute, a compass, and a knife. You probably wouldn't have a radio for communication and would have to travel to a safe zone for pick-up, so navigation was important. They went over all the uses that a parachute had, such as making a hammock to sleep off the ground, a shelter, and the shroud lines could be used for traps and snares. They taught us to make the snares and deadfalls, but stressed that we may go hungry for long periods of time. That was not necessarily life threatening, but going without water would be life threatening. All the ways to find water were discussed and how we should prepare it before drinking. They showed us how to make solar stills and how to make potable water from our own urine.

They stressed the importance of staying healthy. If you became sick or injured, your chances of survival went down exponentially. They taught us how to make splints and how to set our own bones should they become broken. If you parachute out of an airplane in an emergency, you usually don't have time to pick a nice, soft spot to land. It is more likely that you will come down hard in big rocks, trees, or water. Those things hurt really badly. It was very likely that you would be injured once on the ground. The crude techniques we were taught would be painful and possibly disfiguring, but were designed to save our lives.

I can remember one session we had on open wounds. Most likely any cut or gash we received would get infected, and if medication wasn't available, you would likely perish from it. We were taught to let flys land on the wound and allow them to lay eggs in it. In a few days maggots would emerge and would eat the festered flesh. The maggots would not eat good healthy flesh and would begin to fall off the wound when all the putrid flesh was eaten. At that point, you were to eat the maggots. This was serious stuff and all the training sessions were like that.

Next came the really heavy class room stuff taught from experiences of crew members who had been captured. If you were captured, you were in for some really mind-blowing stuff, psychological abuse and physical abuse that was sure to leave permanent scars on you for the rest of your life. They mocked us telling us that we were not tough. If captured, the bad guys would find your weakness immediately and exploit it. They kept telling us how easy it was to be broken and that we had to learn resistance techniques.

They got into an in-depth review of the Code of Conduct, a list of six "articles" created after American POWs suffered at the hands of their captors during the Korean War. They were all tortured using many forms of torture. Many were brainwashed, some even refused to return to the United States after the war. They listed the six "articles" of the Code of Conduct:

1. I am an American fighting in the forces which guard my country and our way of life. I am prepared to give my life in their defense.
2. I will never surrender of my own free will. If in command, I will never surrender the members of my command while they still have the means to resist.
3. If I am captured, I will continue to resist by all means available. I will make every effort to escape and aid others to escape. I will accept neither parole nor special favors from the enemy.
4. If I become a prisoner of war, I will keep faith with my fellow prisoners. I will give no information nor take part in any action which might be harmful to my comrades. If I am senior, I will take command. If not, I will obey the lawful orders of those appointed over me and will back them up in every way.
5. When questioned, should I become a prisoner or war, I am required to give my name, rank, serial number, and date of birth. I will evade answering further questions to the utmost of my ability. I will make no oral or written statements disloyal to my country and its allies or harmful to their cause.
6. I will never forget that I am an American, fighting for freedom, responsible for my actions, and dedicated to

the principles which made my country free. I will trust in my God and in the United States of America.

This is heavy stuff, but it should be what an American believes. The fifth article is the tough one. Keeping your mouth shut when under torture is unbelievably difficult. During the Vietnam War only a few of the prisoners were actually able to do this, and then only partially.

Look at article six. "I will trust my God and in the United States of America." Ask yourself, "In these days and times how many people will I find like this?" I can answer that for you. It is about twenty percent unless you are in the military then it is 100%. If you don't believe it, you don't belong in the service.

Chapter 19 – Prisoner of War Training – Dengler

We went over and over these articles and discussed how they would apply to us if we were in a survival situation. It was important to understand the difficulty that lay before us.

The class room training went on for about ten days, and it was ten grueling days. We knew that crew members were being shot down and captured in Vietnam, but at this time in history we didn't know much about their situations. Also, we did not know the severity of the conditions. There were only one or two cases from the Vietnam era that could be drawn upon for knowledge. These cases were used in the instruction, and, also, since the Instructors were excellent interrogators, they gave us a little taste of what we could expect later in the week. The SERE techniques used by our military are commonly but erroneously believed to have been modeled after abusive Chinese "brain washing" practiced on U.S. POWs during the Korean War, to extract false confessions. Instead most SERE techniques were modeled after 1950's and early 1960's CIA interrogation and psychological warfare practices. The CIA physical and psychological methods were originally codified in the KBARK COUNTERINTELLIGENCE INTERRIGATION MANUAL published in 1963 and were employed in the CIA's Phoenix Program in Vietnam and the CIA's Operation Condor in South America. The other primary source for SERE techniques was 1960's CIA "mind control experiments," using sleep deprivation, drugs, electric shock, isolation, and extended sensory deprivation. Certain of the less physically damaging CIA methods derived from what was at the time called "defensive behavioral research" were reduced and refined as training techniques for the SERE program. Many of these same techniques are still around today.

This was deep and dark stuff, but it would be used on us later to demonstrate how awful being captured can be.

One true account was available at this time. It was the case of Lieutenant Dieter Dengler, the only American ever to break out of a prisoner of war camp in the Laotian jungle and live to tell the tale. Lieutenant Dengler was shot down February 1, 1966 and was finally rescued on July 20, 1966. He had spent seven months running, resisting, and evading. It is a heart breaking story, but all of them are.

On July 20, 1966 Air Force Colonel Eugene Deatrick was flying low over the dangerous Laotian jungle on a bombing mission against the Viet Cong. Colonel Deatrick saw a lone figure below waving to him frantically.

He continued on his flight path, but was puzzled why a native would try to attract his attention. After ten minutes of mulling the situation, he decided to turn back and take another look. That could have been dangerous for him, but something about the guy just did not make sense.

This time around, he saw the letters SOS spelled on a rock in the area. Beside the rock stood an emaciated man dressed in rags, waving the remains of a parachute over his head and signaling desperately.

Colonel Deatrick radioed headquarters, who told him that no Americans had been shot down in the area, and instructed him to carry on with his mission, but the man continued waving, mouthing over and over again: "please don't leave."

No Cong would be able to do that and Deatrick knew something was wrong. Deatrick insisted that rescue helicopters be scrambled. Finally two choppers arrived. One dropped a cable down to the guy and winched him aboard. The chopper crew was very careful because they were afraid they were winching aboard a Viet Cong suicide bomber. As soon as the man was on board, the helicopter crew attacked him, threw him to the deck of the chopper, and searched him. The backpack he had carried only had a half-eaten snake inside. The man was so emaciated and exhausted that he could barely whisper, "I'm an American pilot. Please take me home."

The helicopter crew contacted their base operations and learned that they had rescued Lieutenant Dieter Dengler who had been missing in action and presumed dead. Instead he had been subjected to barbaric torture at the hands of his captors.

By plotting his escape in the tiniest detail over several months, he had escaped his prison by sheer force of will and had survived the mountainous primal Laotian jungle as death stalked his every step.

It was learned that he had deployed from the USS Ranger on February 1, 1960, shortly after becoming engaged to his sweetheart. He was in a formation of three other aircraft on a secret bombing mission near the Laotian border.

Dengler flew for two-and-a-half hours before reaching his target. He rolled his Skyraider into his target run and was immediately strafed by anti-aircraft fire. He heard a loud explosion on his right side that sounded like lightning striking. He looked and his right wing was gone.

The airplane seemed to cartwheel through the sky and there were three more explosions. He was able to guide the plane just enough to crash land in a clearing. This may have saved his life because punching out in dense jungle can hurt you badly.

The landing was so violent that he was thrown one hundred feet from the plane and injured one leg. He lay unconscious for a few minutes before waking and hobbling into the jungle.

The problem with bombing and strafing runs is that you can shoot up grandma and grandpa. This makes everybody really mad, and they take after you with guns, knives, and pitchforks with only one intention, to put as many holes in your body as possible. When you crash nearby the bombing and strafing site, it is always a good idea to run for a long time.

He managed to stay ahead of them for two days. He lived on the run, strapping his injured left leg with bamboo, but finally was caught by the local Pathet Lao, the Laotian equivalent of the communist Viet Cong.

They took him captive and marched him through the jungle all day. At night, he was tied spread-eagle on the ground to four stakes. This exposed him to rats and mosquitoes. In the mornings, his face was so swollen from mosquito bites that he would be unable to see. The Pathet Lao didn't care if the mosquitos sucked all his blood; however, far worse was yet to come.

Knowing this, Dengler made an escape attempt. There was a chase through the jungle for a period of time before he was recaptured near a jungle water hole. This was all that was required for them to begin torture. They would hang him upside down over beds of biting ants. The ants would cover his face with stings until he fainted. At night they suspended him in a cold, damp well. He would be so close to the water that his head would submerge if he went to sleep. Thus began a period of severe sleep deprivation.

Other times he would be dragged by water buffalo whenever they came to a small village. His guards would laugh and goad the water buffalo. It would run through the village dragging him behind to the great amusement of the whole village.

Bloodied and broken, he was asked to sign a document condemning America. If he did sign it, they promised to stop the harsh treatment. He refused. They didn't offer the treat his wounds which began to fester.

One guy made a rope tourniquet around his upper arm. He inserted a piece of wood and twisted until his nerves were cut against his arm bone. The hand was completely unusable for the entire six month period of his captivity.

After some weeks the Pathet Lao handed Dengler over to the even fiercer Viet Cong. As they marched him through a village, a man slipped Dengler's new engagement ring from his finger. Dengler compained to the Viet Cong guards. They found the culprit, summarily chopped off his finger with a machete and threw him aside, handing the ring back to their horrified captive. He said he realized then and there that you don't fool around with the Viet Cong.

Finally Dingler arrived at a prisoner of war camp. He had been looking forward to it, hoping to see other pilots. What he saw horrified him. The first prisoner he saw was carrying his own intestines in his hands.

There were six other captives: four Thais and two fellow Americans, Duane Martin and Eugene DeBruin. One had no teeth. He had been plagued by awful infections and had begged the others to knock them out with a rock and rusty nail in order to release puss from his gums.

They had been there for two and a half years. Dengler realized that he would look like that as well if he didn't escape.

As food began to run low, tension grew between the men. They were given just a single handful of rice to share. The guards had to stalk deer, pulling the grass out of the animal's stomach for the prisoners to eat while they shared the meat.

The prisoners' only treats were snakes they occasionally caught from the communal latrine, or the rats that lived under their hut which they could spear with sharpened bamboo.

Night brought its own misery. The men were handcuffed together and shackled to medieval style foot blocks. They suffered chronic dysentery, and were made to lie in their excrement until morning.

After several months, one of the Thai prisoners heard the guards talking among themselves. The guards were starving too and wanted to return to their villages. They planned to march the captives into the jungle, and shoot them, pretending they had tried to escape.

Dengler convinced the others that they must plan an immediate escape. He planned to attack the guards at lunchtime, when they put down their rifles to eat their food. There was only two minutes and twenty seconds in the day when they could strike. In that time, Dengler had to release all the men from their handcuffs and they had to co-ordinate an attack. It would be close.

The day came and the cook yelled, "Chow time." He got all their handcuffs off and he slipped through the fence and seized three rifles. He ran into the open ready to capture the camp with the help of the other prisoners only to find that the other prisoners had fled leaving him to face the guards. Only Duane had stayed to help him and he was vomiting with nerves.

Dengler raised a machine gun for the first time in his life. He was an air-to-air fighter, not a ground fighter. A guard was only two feet from him rushing at him with a machete. Dengler began firing. He killed five guards while two others ran zigzagging into the jungle. Duane and Dengler had pulled it off. They were out of the prisoner of war camp.

Escape soon brought its own torments. The trek through the dense jungle barefooted was destroying their feet. Their feet were soon mangled from the harsh terrain. They found the sole of one old tennis shoe. They would share the sole strapping it onto a foot with rattan for a few moments respite from the tortuous journey.

They were able to make their way to a fast flowing river. It would be their highway to freedom. They knew it would eventually flow into the Mekong River which would take them over the border into Thailand and safety.

The two men built a raft and floated downstream through ferocious rapids, tying themselves to trees at night. By morning they would be covered in mud and hundreds of leeches.

So weak that they could barely crawl up the river bank, the men eventually reached a settlement, but the villagers were far from welcoming.

The pair knelt on the ground and pleaded for help. One man had a machete in his hands which he swung and hit Duane's leg. Blood gushed everywhere but the man was not through. He made one more swipe and Duane's head came flying off.

Dengler reached for the rubber sole still attached to Duane's foot, grabbed it and ran. He said that from that moment on all his motions became mechanical. He no longer cared if he lived or died.

He began to be followed by this beautiful bear. The bear became like a pet dog and was the only friend he had. He had learned a valuable lesson that the Instructors hammered at us relentlessly. The most dangerous thing out there is man. If you can avoid human contact, you may live and survive.

Dengler said that the next hours and days were his darkest hour. He was on the run again and was little more than a walking skeleton. He floated in and out of hallucination.

He said he got too weak to walk and was crawling along on his belly when he had a vision. These enormous doors opened and lots of horses came galloping out. They were not driven by death but by angels. He knew then that death didn't want him.

It was five days later that Dengler heard the airplane overhead, and the rest is history, well, almost history. After he was rescued, he was taken into the hospitalized care of the CIA who wanted to interrogate him and learn as much as possible from him.

His fellow crew mates learned that he had been rescued but was being held and interrogated by the CIA. They commandeered a helicopter from the flight deck of their carrier and carried out a raid on the CIA's headquarters kidnapping Dengler in his bed, putting him aboard the helicopter, and flying him back to his carrier, where he was given a hero's welcome.

At night, however, he was tormented by awful terrors and had to be tied to his bed. In the end, his friends put him to sleep in a cockpit surrounded by pillows. It was the only place he felt safe. Sadly, he recovered physically, but never completely put the ordeal out of his mind.

The man's ordeal was what we had to look forward to if we got shot down in Vietnam.

Chapter 20 – Hoa Lo Eleven

By 1973 other stories were coming to light, like the eleven G.I.'s in the Hanoi Hilton that the V.C. could not totally break. One was Navy Commander James Bond Stockdale. On September 9, 1965 he was flying his A-4 Skyhawk on a mission over North Vietnam when his plane took enemy fire and hurled down. Forced to eject with seconds to spare, he sustained severe injuries: his left leg bent sideways by 60 degrees and his kneecap was smashed. His left shoulder was dislocated which rendered his left arm useless. He also thought his back was broken.

Stockdale was quickly discovered by villagers, who beat him and dragged him through the streets until he was delivered to his ultimate destination: the Hoa Lo prison, or, as it was derisively known among American POW's held there, the Hanoi Hilton.

Twenty five months later, Stockdale was the highest ranking Naval officer in captivity and would be moved, along with ten other American POW's to an even more remote prison site they called Alcatraz.

Together these men were regarded by the Vietnamese as the most dangerous, subversive, and indestructible Americans they had ever encountered. Their plan was to isolate them from other POW's, and each other, hoping to finally maintain some control over these most insolent American soldiers. Things did not go according to plan.

On February 11, 1965 Lt. Commander Bob Shumaker became the second U.S. pilot shot down over Vietnam.

He was taken to the Hanoi Hilton and held in isolation for four months before he was allowed to write home.

In that time Shumaker, known as Shu, made contact with one other POW. Shu had seen another American regularly dumping his slop bucket outside and managed to scratch out a note on a piece of toilet paper.

"Welcome to the Hanoi Hilton," he wrote. "If you get this note, scratch your balls as you are coming back." Shu then smuggled the note into a crack in the wall near the latrine, and just a few minutes later, his fellow American walked through the courtyard furiously scratching his balls. He managed to leave a reply: He was Ron Storz, Captain USAF.

As more American POW's arrived, Shu realized that the Vietnamese would soon isolate them. How could they keep communicating? Morse code was no good, even North Vietnamese understood that. Then he remembered a tap code developed by American POW's in Korea, one he had learned in SERE.

This was how the Americans at Hanoi, led by Stockdale would communicate. They could warn each other about the most sadistic guards, check in with each other, relay what to expect in interrogation, encourage each other not to break, offer consolation when, one by one, they eventually did.

There was Harry Jenkins, a six-foot-five Navy pilot who refused to give up what his father did for a living. He knew that once they got that, they would want more and more. Jenkins was tortured so brutally he was sure he would lose his hands. He passed out and when he came to, his tormentors hung him from his wrists, still tied behind his back, from a meat hook. He had never conceived of such pain. He asked

God to take him. Again Jenkins passed out. When he came to again he was made to kneel on gravel for hours, and only when the meat was sheared from his kneecaps did he submit. "My father grows flowers," he told them.

The torture was constant. The Americans were thrown in tiny cells, slabs of concrete for beds, single, bare light bulbs making sleep impossible. They were in a constant state of starvation, and when they were fed, their watery soup was laced with pebbles or feces. They were made to stand on stacked stools for days on end. They were often strapped down by 15-pound leg irons, which caused lacerations and infection, or by stocks at the ends of their beds, which kept them on their backs for days. The walls and floors were overrun with roaches and rats. When they were strapped down, they were forced to lie in their own excrement.

Jim Stockdale, who had been held in isolation for 18 months, worried when he saw the Vietnamese begin to soften toward their prisoners. The beatings lessened, the food increased. This was equally dangerous, and could cause POW's to submit: to confess to war crimes which would be used for propaganda, to give up fellow soldiers in exchange for release-the "Fink Release Program," Stockdale called it.

Stockdale's second in command was Commander Jerry Denton, who had been hauled before T.V. cameras by the North Vietnamese and had blinked "t-o-r-t-u-r-e" in Morse code on the air.

There was Nels Tanner, tortured into writing a confession of war crimes; he identified a Lt. Clark Kent and was thereafter known as the author of Superman's confession.

While transported to Hanoi after being shot down, Jim Mulligan's captors poured gasoline over his bound arms, fusing threads of rope into his wounds. Howie Rutledge was beaten mercilessly during his first day in captivity; refusing to give his ship and squadron. He was told to get on the floor, and a guard thrashed his injured and dislocated leg until it pressed flat on the ground. He and Sam Johnson both suffered over 60 boils each during one summer, and Johnson had been held in solitary multiple times, often going six days in a row without sunlight.

Ron Storz had been made to stand on a stool for seven days straight then beaten nearly to death with a bamboo stick. Hands tied behind his back, George McKnight was held for 34 nights in an air raid trench four feet long; he was 6-foot-two. He would conspire with POW George Coker, and together they would make a daring escape from the Hanoi Hilton in 1967, getting 15 miles before they were discovered by villagers on a river bank.

Together, these eleven men were the most unbreakable prisoners at the Hanoi Hilton, so the Vietnamese moved them to a remote outpost, the one the POW's called Alcatraz. Here in a small structure near the Ministry of Defense, the Alcatraz eleven were each thrown, one by one, into windowless rooms. Stockdale and Mulligan were considered so dangerous that the Vietnamese left an empty cell between them, to thwart any secret communication.

It didn't work. Mulligan scratched audible messages while he was at the latrine. The two men, isolated from the other nine, figured out that they could flash hand signals through camp in the gap between the door and the floor. These messages were often no more subversive than, "How are you doing?"-

words of solace or encouragement. Sometimes, they would tap codes to signal group prayer, or the Pledge of Allegiance, which they would whisper simultaneously.

Despite increased isolation, starvation, and torture, the men remained determined. By spring 1968, the men had spent five months at Alcatraz, and the cells were becoming sweatboxes, reaching up to 110 degrees each day. The combined stench of human waste and sweat made it nearly impossible to breathe, yet Stockdale and Denton refused to capitulate. Instead, they ordered their men to join a hunger strike. Denton was soon called to meet with a commander they had dubbed Rat.

"I want to congratulate you," Denton said, "on putting us to a slow death by heat."

"No, Denton," said Rat, "I did not know conditions were that bad. Our orders are to keep you isolated and in irons. We have no orders to kill you. We will study." That did not mean an end to the torture, yet the men remained united. On the third anniversary of his capture, Stockdale found a message at the latrine, which read in part, "We love you."

Two months later, after Nixon was elected, the Vietnamese wanted real propaganda out of the Alcatraz eleven. They beat George McKnight for 36 hours straight; then beat and tortured Denton so brutally his arms turned black; Jim Mulligan was strung up and beaten for six days and Nels Tanner was beaten for 17 days. Sam Johnson was so brutalized that when he finally submitted, he literally could not write the apology demanded by the Vietnamese. He was only able to sign it, and when he was thrown back in his cell, he heard Jerry Denton whisper to him from his adjacent cell, "Sam, Sam, its O.K. Buddy."

"I made them write it, Jerry," he replied, "But I had to sign it."

"It's O.K. Sam," Jerry said, "You are O.K. Hang on. You did good."

Each of the men would break, and each of the men understood. In fact, all of them worried most about Ron Storz, who had been in isolation for four years and had tried to commit suicide with a razor. Jerry Denton urged Storz to say whatever he had to so he could get out of isolation. His life was in danger, and it wasn't a violation of the Code of Conduct.

Storz was too far gone to take it as anything but an insult. He was the only one who wouldn't make it back. He died in captivity.

On December 9, 1969, after 25 months, the POW's were taken out of Alcatraz and transported back to the Hanoi Hilton. By now, the families of POW's had brought enough publicity to the cause, forcing the U.S. government to address it, that the North Vietnamese did not want to be caught violating the Geneva Convention. They were not freed from the Hanoi Hilton until February 17, 1973. Two weeks after the Paris Peace Accords.

Not only did every Alcatraz survivor go on to have a full and happy life, several continued to serve the country that had sent them into this misguided war. Tanner, Jenkins, Rutledge, Mulligan, Coker, McKnight, and Johnson went back to active duty. Johnson served in Congress. Shumaker and Denton retired as Rear Admirals and Denton also served in the Senate. Stockdale ultimately ran for Vice President on the ticket with Ross Perot.

Chapter 21 – Ted Ballard

Lt. Col. Ted Ballard of Spartanburg, S.C. was also held as a prisoner of war. He was a prisoner for over six years and imprisoned in a building the Americans called Pig Sty. Ballard was beaten so badly by the Vietnamese that he ended up in a full body cast. Ballard was nursed back to health by fellow inmate George McSwain.

The Vietnamese demanded that Ballard confess to war crimes which would have been used as propaganda against America. Ballard refused and in retaliation the Vietnamese took McSwain away and tortured him. They forced McSwain to spend 16 hours a day with his hands over his head. When Ballard told McSwain that he would write a confession to save McSwain from torture, McSwain refused, instead opting for more torture instead. McSwain's torture went on for seven weeks with him standing with his arms over his head for 16 hours each day and getting severe beatings every other day.

Ballard and his fellow prisoners would communicate using the prisoner of war code taught in SERE. The Vietnamese tortured them severely if they were caught communicating by code. The men encouraged each other to follow the Code of Conduct and endured as much torture as they could before breaking mentally and physically.

The men were tortured for holding religious services in their cells, but eventually the Vietnamese relented and allowed the prisoners to hold services for 15 minutes while the guards stood over them with bayonets at the ready.

Another prisoner, Mike Christian, made a small American flag and hid it in his cell. When the guards weren't around, the prisoners would salute the flag and sing "God Bless America." The guards eventually found the flag and beat Christian severely. He had to be nursed back to health by his fellow prisoners. The day after his beating, Christian began making another flag.

This is all very heavy and dark stuff. We went over situations like this in our training with the Instructors telling us we had to remain true to the Code of Conduct. To capitulate would be to give the enemy material which could be used against America in the news media.

As I write these passages, I can't help but reflect upon current situations. Democrats are rioting in cities across the country. Republicans acting like babies. Veterans denied simple benefits at V.A. Hospitals such as drug coverage or simple health care. Has this country no conscience? Where is our national decency? Men and women in military uniforms are forced to the very limits of human endurance to protect a bunch of self-centered crybabies. Come on people, grow up. Say something positive. Say something nice. Help an old lady. This is America, by far the best, most prosperous country in the world. Act responsibly. Act like you deserve it. Don't be lazy and live off your relatives. Work for your bread. Find God. It's in the Military Code of Conduct. Military personnel, still living today, have been beaten and tortured because they wanted to pray to God. Liberals, you should stand ashamed. Don't point fingers at the other person. Your finger should point toward your own heart. Your country and your way of life are at risk. Unite under one cause, to be decent human beings. Self- centered behavior needs to end.

Chapter 22 – POW Camp

Class finally ended for us and we were marched to the supply room to get more gear for further training. We were given cold weather clothing, heavy parkas, two sleeping bags, and a poncho. We were told to dress in the clothing and bring our sleeping bags and ponchos outside and deposit them on the ground. It was now dark and very cold, well below freezing.

This all looked a little strange. I was getting hungry. Where was chow? I never missed a meal unless it was an emergency. My days of living on the edge as a child had marked me. Maybe some kind sergeant would pass out cookies. No such luck. This was the military. They believed that you needed an example if you were to learn, and they believed that it had to be repeated seven times for you to remember it. Here we go!

Gun shots rang out! People began to scream! Chaos reigned supreme! Our Instructors, who, unbeknown to us were actually paid informants for the enemy, ran up and told us that we were under attack from the bad guys. The only avenue of escape was to crawl under an obstacle course to get to the other side to safety. The only problem with this little ruse was that the obstacle course was actually barbed wire laced about eighteen inches above the ground and covered a very long distance. They told us that we would have to crawl fast because the enemy had just broken the perimeter and was headed our way. If we didn't get to the safe zone, we would be killed. To add emphasis to the chaos, gunshots began to reverberate close overhead.

Down we went, and we began crawling for our lives. We were flat on our bellies unable to rise higher because of the barbed wire. In order to go forward you had to pull with your elbows and push with your knees and toes. Adding to the discomfort was the cold temperatures and the yelling, screaming, and gunfire. I could see muzzle flashes over my right shoulder. We crawled and crawled. The skin was beginning to chafe and rub off my elbows and knees. I have always sworn that we crawled for at least a mile that night. I really don't know how far it was, but it was calculated to be long enough to leave a person, who was in good shape, completely winded when finished.

When we stumbled out the other side and were trying to get our bearings, we were surprised to learn that our collaborators had deceived us and the enemy was waiting on us. We were taken captive and rough housed on the way to prison where I was blindfolded and led to a cell. The blindfold was removed and I was slammed into my cell which resembled a wooden casket stood on end with a door that locked from outside. I was slammed hard into my prison cell and the door was slammed shut and locked from outside. There was yelling and people screaming in pain in the room in which my cell was located. It was as dark as the inside of a tomb in this cell. I had to take inventory of my situation by feel, which was fairly easy to do. Both shoulders touched a wall and the wall was still tight, even to my hips. My back was flat against the back wall, and I was pressed as tightly against it as I could get. If I didn't stay pressed against the back wall, my face would rub on the door which had been unceremoniously slammed on my nose. Every few minutes the guard would come by my cell and beat on the door with the butt of his rifle. I could feel the blows on the door because the wood would bend inward just enough to hit the tip of my nose. The position was cramped and anyone with claustrophobia would go insane. There must have been several of those because I could hear people begging to be released; however, it could have been the collaborators adding to our stress. We never knew.

I spent hours in this tiny cell. I had to stand at attention or my knees would rub on the door. If the guard slammed the door with your knees on it then broken kneecaps were expected. The stress of holding one position for a long period of time does something to you psychologically. I began to see things, very scary things. This was physical stress aided by sleep deprivation. We had been in class all day, then forced to crawl forever, and, now, it must be close to dawn and I had had no rest whatsoever.

The first things I saw were the spiders. Although it was pitch black inside my cell, I could see spiders. They were as big as my hand and they were hairy like a tarantula. One time I witnessed a tarantula jump waist high trying to jump on a guy. Ever since then, I had been wary of the things. The tarantulas were the very things coming for me now. Remember, I was not asleep and dreaming. I was wide awake and had normal reasoning powers, but I was seeing big, hairy spiders coming toward my eyes. I tried to move away from them, but the small cell was just like being tied head to toe. I couldn't move, and they were beginning to bow-up their backs getting ready to spring on my eyes.

The guard must have heard me moving around in there, scraping the wood with my clothing because the door suddenly flew open. Light from outside flooded my senses and I was blinded and fell forward to the floor. The guard yanked me to my feet and slammed me into a wall. He told me that I was "War Criminal number one five" and that I should refer to myself as such. We had no names anymore. We had committed war crimes and had no rights. He pointed to a tin can in the corner and explained that was my "sanitary facility" in the event I had to use the bathroom, but I was not to use it without permission. Besides, now was not my allotted time.

I was thrown across the room and bullied into an area that contained a small box that could be broken down into a bottom, four sides, and a top. It looked to be no more than a cubic foot in volume.

He screamed at me to sit on the bottom part of the box in a fetal position and place my arms along my legs with my palms facing upward, what he called the "po-seesh." "Get in po-seesh!" he yelled. I assumed this was bad guy speech for position. After pushing and shoving and kicking, he got me into a position that suited him with my head bent all the way down so that my chin was touching my ankles. Then he began to assemble the box around me. The back came up and pushed into my back, both sides came up and were roughly pushed against my shoulders. The front came up and slammed against the back of my head. The top came down and crashed across the top of my back and my neck. Then I heard him padlock the thing. It was total darkness again.

If I thought my cell was tight, then this was beyond belief. I could feel the tendons all over my body screaming in pain. You couldn't move even half an inch. I prayed that I wouldn't see the spiders again. The position was bad enough; I didn't need hallucinations to go with it. Then he began to roll the thing and slam it with the butt of his rifle. I became dizzy and disorientated, not knowing what position I had stopped rolling, but knowing that each one hurt worse than the first. This went on and on. I could feel my shoulder joints begin to slide out of place. Things began to go completely numb. I lost feeling in my hands and feet and my head swam sickeningly.

Suddenly, the lock was release and the box fell apart around me, but I couldn't move. I was like a lump of clay molded into a cube, unable to relax.

Again, the rough treatment began, dragging me along the floor screaming at me to "get up and walk." Finally able to stagger, I stumbled along in front of him, being pushed and shoved, until I was slammed back into my cell.

It was still pitch dark in my cell. My real eyes could see nothing, but my hallucinogenic eyes saw a lot. I could see a spacious room just off my right shoulder, and it contained a luxurious bed, but my body couldn't move toward it.

As I stood there wondering what would happen next, a wide variety of psyops stuff began to blare through the speaker mounted in the outside room. It was scratchy and sounded third-worldish and blew out a mind-numbing cacophony of out of control saxophone followed by Rudyard Kipling reciting his poem "Boots" over and over in a haunting outer worldly voice. Have somebody read this stupid poem to you ten thousand times and try not to go insane in the process. It had two psychological purposes: 1) It drove you nuts, and 2) It kept you from relaxing and dozing, adding to the sleep deprivation.

Occasionally instructions from the guards were piped over the speaker, for instance, the rules for heeding calls of nature: "War criminals wishing to use the sanitary facilities must ask permission by saying, "War criminal numbering whatever wishes to urinate or defecate." Do not do so until you are told to do so."

At some point a guard opened my cell door, blindfolded me, and led me to an interview with the camp commander. I can't remember much of my interview, but I looked up an encounter by someone who recently graduated from the class. His encounter was much like mine, and I will quote his story.

"The camp commander's friendly demeanor led me to believe this was the "soft sell" portion of my interrogation. He asked me how I was feeling. I joked I was hungry. He looked concerned and said he would get me some hot food right after I got back to my cell. I also joked that the music was terrible and I'd prefer the Beatles, and he said he would make that happen right away.

Then he asked me where I was stationed. I said I couldn't answer that. He asked me what kind of airplanes I flew. I said I couldn't answer that either. After a second round of refusals his friendly mood shifted to anger, and he ordered the guard to take me back to my cell, saying I was "insincere" and needed to see the provost marshal for further "re-edu-ma-cation."

Another extended stay in solitary confinement in my cell accompanied by "Boots" on the repeat, I was blindfolded again and taken to another part of the camp. As I was led through the snow I heard a loud banging and people screaming. Once inside the building, my blindfold was removed and one of the guards told me to climb into a small box, barely big enough for me to fit.

Once I'd wedged myself in, the guard slammed the lid. He instructed me that when he banged on the box once I was to yell my war criminal number, and when he banged twice I was to yell my social security number. This went on for a while, and fortunately I didn't get claustrophobic, because, if I did, the confined space would have freaked me out.

The box treatment was followed by some "up and jumps," known to the rest of us as jumping jacks, and other calisthenics punctuated by guards slapping me and throwing me to the floor. When I was good and winded a guard led me to a room where a big burly man with a red beard was waiting.

Red Beard asked me a few questions about my military profile, and each time I didn't answer, he slapped me. He produced an American flag and threw it on the ground and told me to dance on it. I tried to avoid it but he pushed me and I wound up stepping on the flag and as I did a photographer appeared and snapped a shot.

After another round of questions I didn't answer, Red Beard decided it was time for stronger measures. He pushed me to the floor and made me sit on my hands. He straddled my legs as he fired up some pipe tobacco and started blowing smoke in my face using a large rubber tube. I couldn't breathe. The room started spinning. My head hit the floor and I puked. To my horror, even though I hadn't finished puking, Red Beard blew more smoke in my face.

This felt like real torture, and I was convinced he was going to kill me. As I fought to get a breath of air, I managed to beg him to stop and offered to tell him something, hoping to employ the techniques where you try to bend but not break by throwing some meaningless bullshit.

I told him I was stationed in Florida even though I was really stationed in Virginia and that I flew helicopters even though I flew jets. Red Beard laughed and called the guard back in, telling him to give me as much food and water as I wanted because I had been helpful.

As I was led back to my cell, I felt like a total fool who had caved in too easily.

After another period in isolation with my moral at an all- time low, a guard came and led me back to the camp commander's office. The camp commander told me about a junior enlisted man who had gone through the same torture, but, instead of talking, he had come off the floor screaming "Article Five," a reference to the Code of Conduct where it states a POW should only give name, rank, and date of birth. "You are supposed to be an officer, but an enlisted man is stronger than you," he said. "And you are insincere. You told us wrong information. I'm sending you back to provost."

Sure enough, after more time in my cell to contemplate my short comings as an officer, I was back in front of Red Beard. I hated the sight of Red Beard. I felt another emotion that was like an epiphany: I wasn't about to let America down again. The nation depended on me to be strong. That is why I had a good education and they had put me through flight school. Seriously, all these things were running through my mind. If I had to die, so be it. Let the smoke blow.

After some more passing out and puking followed by more passing out and puking, Red Beard let me go.

The next day we were let out of solitary confinement and forced to do hard labor around camp where our tasks included carving a "heli-mo-copter pad" in the ice covered ground, an impossible task for which we were beaten for our lack of progress. One guy was stripped to his underwear and forced to stand at attention as his clothes were burned in front of him.

The camp commander gathered us together, and holding a Bible aloft, told us our beliefs were bullshit and that the only religious figure Americans truly worshipped was St. Walt Disney. He threw the Bible down and stomped it, which caused some of the prisoners to react enough that the guards felt obliged to slap them and throw them to the ground.

The cycle of hard labor in the freezing cold followed by "re-edu-ma-cation" cycles on the propaganda machine went on for hours and hours, until the sun was about to set on our miserable existence once more. Morale was low. We were sure we were never getting out of there and our lives as we knew them were over.

Suddenly there was a burst of gunfire and a group of guys in cammies rappelled over the walls of the compound at various spots. They took the camp personnel into custody and announced that they were Navy Seals. The Stars and Stripes was hoisted on the flag pole and the National Anthem played over the P.A.

There wasn't a dry eye among us as we sang along. We were Americans, and we were free again.

The Senate Intelligence Committee's recent report on the CIA's enhanced torture techniques during the early years in Iraq and Afghanistan has restarted discussions about DoD's methods and where they are taught and learned. The SERE school curriculum has been lumped into those discussions.

For me SERE wasn't about torture. It was about the realization that the pomp and ceremony, the pageantry and adulation that surrounds wearing a military uniform was meaningless without the courage and commitment that under pins them.

SERE taught me a big lesson in sacking up, and I can say that it was, in fact, the most important school I ever attended."

From the point of meeting Red Beard for the first time until the last sentence above, you have been reading an account from another man, mainly because my memory is fuzzy on these items, but my experiences were very similar, and my emotions closely paralleled his.

I was in this prisoner camp all of one night, all the next day, and all of the next night, all without any sleep or rest and always under duress. This had been followed by a day in class and a mad dash through an obstacle course which left me exhausted. In all I had been awake for 48 hours, much of which had been some form of CIA enhanced torture. I had suffered fatigue, stress, betrayal, torture, and hallucinations. Now I was left with the realization of how easy it had been for them. My mind said, "You should have been tougher," but my mind had betrayed me as well and had taken me to places I had never been before. Now I truly knew just how tough I really was and it scared me. You grow up thinking of yourself as some mighty hero only to find out just the opposite. If you think of yourself as being grandiose and above everyone else, I suggest that you build up enough balls to go through this school.

Another thing the prison taught me was that someday some bunch of crazy Americans will scale a wall, kill everybody, and take you home. If you were not true to yourself and your men while in prison, then the angst that follows your return will be much worse than the prison camp. That is the reason for the Code of Conduct and why it is so important to follow it, even to death.

You would think that the story would end here, but it doesn't. The most difficult part was yet to come!

Chapter 23 – Joe King

Our rescuers told us that we had to hurry and grab our sleeping bags and ponchos and meet them out front. We were going to come under attack from hostiles, and we have to escape. We would be taken to a remote area that could be guarded by night, but we would be on our own during the days that followed. Safe sites would be situated in different locations in the mountains and we would have to find them in order to be safe each night. If we were caught, the bad guys would return us to the prison camp, and we could expect even worse treatment at their hands.

Holy Crap! I had had enough of this prison camp, so I grabbed my equipment and boarded a blue school bus. We set off on a long trip through a wild and mountainous region. There were no houses, few roads, and no animals-nothing. I was so tired that I fell asleep sitting upright in the seat and didn't awaken until the bus bumped to a halt. We bailed out and were met by a couple so called friendlies who would show us woodsmen skills before night fall.

Our education in how to become Daniel Boone began immediately.

We had been issued a small amount of equipment. We had two sleeping bags – Government Issue, green camo, non-waterproof, heavy – hooded rubber poncho that smelled bad, a compass – SE CC 4580 Military/Linsatic/Prismatic sighting w/pouch – a hooded coyote fur lined cold weather coat, heavy gloves, a fish hook with three feet of string, and an onion. We had already been told to bring our own knife. I had a k-bar case knife sharpened like a razor. That was it. Daniel Boone traveled light.

There were about twenty people in our group plus the two friendlies. They told us that we would be safe as a group for the night but soon we must separate and travel in pairs. A group was too easy to spot.

They began the process of separating us into pairs. Somehow, I got paired with old Joe King. I was thrilled. Joe and I had gone to Pilot Training together, and I knew him pretty well. I was married and had lived off base in Laredo and Joe was a bachelor and had lived in the Bachelor's Officer's Quarters on base. Joe was an ol' boy from Tennessee and had the easy southern drawl that I was brought up with. He was also a scamp, a very mischievous fellow. He would make a great travel partner.

As they announced the pairings and Joe discovered he was paired with me, he didn't seem to share my enthusiasm about the pairing. Somehow he seemed to know intuitively that the devil followed around in my footprints and had a habit of jumping out scaring everybody in sight sometimes. The look Joe gave me was somewhat obtuse and wary. I didn't let that bother me particularly. I knew that I had a tough guy for a partner and could expect to finish this school without further mishap.

Old Joe was a lanky, likeable guy who just seemed to bring out the best in people – even me. The thing I always remembered about him was that he had big blue eyes that were distinguishable from a distance. Most people don't have eyes like that. Anyway, he didn't complain too much, and we paired off watching the demonstrations, but before I begin, I feel the need to describe the country side we were in because it was unique and would become our worst nightmare.

Chapter 24 – What It Looked Like

We were in the Colville National Forest high in the mountains in the third week of October, and snow was already lying in patches on the ground.

Colville covers 1.1 million acres of remote wilderness and lies along the borders of Washington, Idaho, and British Columbia. It lies along the 49th parallel, north latitude, so it is pretty far north.

It was first shaped more than 10,000 years ago by Ice Age glaciers that carved three major valleys of today's Columbia River.

The major rivers in the forest follow paths that were bulldozed by the glaciers. The ice sheets were a mile high. They surged south out of Canada and covered all but the tallest peaks several times during the last two million years. The ice ground the sharp edges so they became smooth, leaving the mountains rounded.

The rivers that formed in these valleys were the Columbia, San Poil Curlew, and the Pend Oreille (pronounced "ponderay"). The last two rivers flow north into Canada before entering the Columbia. The 1.1 million acres roll like high seas. Three waves of mountains run from north to south separated by through-valleys. These ranges – the Okanogan, Kettle River, and Selkirk – are considered foothills of the Rocky Mountains.

We were making our camp tucked among the Selkirk Mountains in the extreme northeastern corner of Washington, the U – shaped 43,348 acre Salmo –Priest Wilderness which extends its borders along those of Idaho and British Columbia. Its two most prominent features are two very long ridges, generally running southwest to northeast, connected toward their northern ends by a ridge crowned by 6,828 – foot Salmo Mountain. The eastern ridge stands lower, more wooded, more rounded-off and more accessible than the steep-sided, rocky crested western ridge. Streams have cut deep drainages into both ridges; water from the eastern side ends up in Idaho's Priest River. The remaining wilderness drains generally westerly via Sullivan Creek and the Salmo River into the Pend Oreille River.

Below the ridge tops of this well-watered wilderness (at 50 plus inches of precipitation annually) you'll find the largest growth of virgin forest left in eastern Washington. The forest houses mule deer, white-tailed deer, elk, black bears, cougars, bobcats, badgers, pine martins, lynx, Bighorn sheep, and moose. Though rarely sighted, threatened and endangered species, including woodland caribou, grizzly bears, and gray wolves also roam. Winter snows begin in mid-October and blanket the ground until early July.

There are several different types of forests in the area. Dry forests dominate the lowest elevations, about 20% of the refuge. These forests are comprised of Ponderosa Pines and Douglas fir and can withstand hotter, drier conditions and frequent fire. Both species develop thick bark which protects the large mature trees from fire damage. Grand fir can also be present in some areas. Pine grass, service berry, snowberry, and ceanothus dominate the understory. These stands can be quite long-lived and productive but tend to regenerate slowly because of fire frequency and dry conditions.

Moist forests are dominated by Douglas fir, grand fir, and western hemlock. Lodge pole pines, western white pine, western larch, and Engelmann spruce are also present in these mid-level forests. This zone receives more precipitation and can support denser forests than the dry forest. Understory species include ninebark, huckleberry, spirea, and snowberry.

Cold forests cover the highest ridges with Engelmann spruce and subalpine fir. Other species are western larch, Douglas fir, western hemlock, lodge pole pine, western white pine, and grand fir. Rates of growth are slow and nutrients are limited. Standing dead or down trees may persist for a long time because cool temperatures slow decomposition. Bunchberry, dogwood, azalea, twin flower, and huckleberry are understory species.

Today's landscape emerged from the melting ice about 10,000 years ago. Animals and plants followed the retreating glaciers northward and humans were not far behind. The first Indians probably began hunting, fishing, and gathering in the area about 9,000 years ago.

Archeologists estimate that the Indians caught more than 1,000 salmon a day at Kettle Falls during peak runs. Salmon congregated below the wide, low falls on the way upstream to spawn. The Indian fishermen stood on rocks and wooden platforms to spear and net the fish as they jumped up through the whitewater. Indians, camped near the falls, smoked and dried the fish, preserving it for winter use. Runners would carry the smoked fish back to the elders and young children who had remained behind in their winter villages.

By 1826 American fur traders were living in Fort Colville, built near Kettle Falls. This restricted the Indian's ability to fish the falls for their winter survival.

Kettle Falls and the salmon run disappeared under the rising water of Roosevelt Reservoir in the 1930's when a new dam was built.

Joe and I gazed upon this landscape in shocked awe. We were both from the South. We felt as if we had been picked-up and transported to Mars.

At first glance, the land looked ancient and convoluted, but upon closer inspection, there was lots of younger growth, both trees and vegetation. I had never seen any of the trees or any of the vegetation before. It was all new to me.

Fires, spawned by lightning strikes, sweep through these ancient mountains during dry periods. The fire sweeps up and down the mountains faster than an elk can run, and only the lucky animals survive. The vegetation isn't so lucky for it is burned to destruction by the fast, raging infernos, but the vegetation has a fall-back position. It uses the calcium and nitrous oxides in the ash as food for new growth, and the forests and meadows spring-back healthier than before the fire; all the dense forest undergrowth (understory) gets burned away leaving plenty of room for expansion of new growth. The natural fertilizer from the ash adds fervor to the growth, and the new trees seem destined to grow taller than their predecessors, and are green and happy.

Hidden in the growth patterns were huge deadfalls left from the fires. The large trees do not fall completely, but they are killed. Wind and rain push them over and they slide downhill piling-up in large mounds that can be as high as a two story house and over one hundred feet across. If they don't wash into big piles, they are still lying in all directions, partially disguised by the new growth. Wolves can glide over these downed giants in easy, loping strides, but humans have to struggle over one downed giant only to face another a short distance away. Humans don't glide over this landscape like a wolf.

Since we were at such a high latitude, the sun always seems about to set, even early in the day; the slant of the sun's rays is different and shadows always look longer. This makes judging distance tricky. It is also difficult to gauge time because the shadows don't shorten and lengthen.

As I looked at the forests, they were not deciduous but evergreen, and they are patchy. There can be large patches of trees that are so thick that you can hardly force your body through them, and, suddenly, these will open onto wide vistas that are essentially treeless. In these open areas, you can study the surroundings over long distances and determine if your course is correct, but the actual distance from one place to another is deceptive. A spot that looks to be a mile away can take half a day to traverse.

In many areas the trees that are standing and growing may only be twelve inches in diameter and fifty feet high, spaced closely together, while the dead trees lying about may be three feet in diameter and one hundred feet long.

The earth was a grayish tan and had a crumbly friable texture. Plants, when you see them, are growing in individual groups with open spaces between the groups as if a master gardener had spaced all the plants on the 1.1 million acres. When it is warm, alpine flowers in white, oranges, and blues dot the landscape. In winter, when snow is on the ground, these open areas between tree patches are beautiful snow areas, unbroken by bush growth. In winter all you see is green conifers, fallen trees, rocks, and snow. The snow will lie on the broad, green boughs of the conifers like it was being held out on a shovel and will stay there unless the wind blows or something shakes the trees.

The rocks that you see all around are light gray and are everywhere. They range from fist-sized to the size of a small house. Like the plants, they seem to have been scattered carefully by the master gardener who had the perfect eye for form and symmetry.

I took special note of the topography. It was either uphill or downhill. Sometimes it was gentle, rolling areas, and other times it was steep and sheer. In traveling the area, you seem to get an equal mixture of both and large amounts that are somewhere between the two extremes; however, walking a straight line from point A to point B is never easy. Most of the time you feel like you are walking on the roof of a house, each step requiring an inordinate amount of exertion.

The air was cold and thin. It goes into your lungs in great gulps but doesn't transfer much oxygen. You have to become accustomed to traveling in these conditions and learn to pace yourself; otherwise, you may become dizzy, and disorientated, unable to use your cogitative skills to solve problems. A condition such as that can be deadly for a pilgrim in this wilderness.

The sky doesn't appear as deep blue as it appears closer to the equator. It stays a lighter color of blue, sometimes very bright and other times hazy with high clouds.

Chapter 25 – Outdoor Lore

With my observations of my surroundings over, I began to pay closer attention to the demonstrations that the friendlies were giving us. As with all Military Schools, you generally get one crack at a practice run; after that, you may be totally on your own.

They were demonstrating how to make a quick, effective shelter. Since both partners wore a waterproof poncho, the easiest shelter was one made from the ponchos. First you marked a spot on the ground just big enough to cover two bodies, about six feet by six feet. Next you went to the nearest conifer and began breaking off the tips of the branches, about eighteen inches in length. The branches were then stuck into the ground with the tips pointed upward and very close together. This made a small airspace between the snow and your back. Next we took off our ponchos and snapped one side of the first poncho to one side of the second poncho. That became our tent. We would throw the ponchos over a rope tied between two trees and off the ground by about two feet. That made a tent that would keep the snow off you. Next, we each stuffed one sleeping bag inside the other bag so that we had a double layered sleeping apparatus and tossed them under the ponchos, side by side. Now we had a home for the night. It only took two people about thirty minutes to construct. The friendlies stressed over and over the importance of having everything dry before we got into our sleeping bags. They said that if the sleeping bags weren't completely dry that you would freeze to death inside your bag. It was also important that you dried your clothing at night before going to bed, no matter how much trouble it was or how long it took. Cold is transported by moisture and frostbite would be guaranteed if you slept in wet clothes. In fact, they said that we had to dry our sleeping bag, then dry our clothes, and sleep naked inside the sleeping bag. I noticed Joe looking at me out of the corner of his eye as if he weren't completely sure about something. He was a suspicious cuss.

The next most important thing was navigation. We went over the fine points of using a topographical map and a compass. The trick is to get your compass lined-up with magnetic north. Then you line your compass up with the way you want to travel and sit it on the map. The direction the compass is pointing across the map is your direction. As long as you triangulate your exact position on the map, you will know exactly what is ahead of you and how far it is to it. It also will tell you elevation so you will know if you are traveling up, down, or level. The map would show streams and lakes. The only things the map didn't show was deadfalls, rocks, bogs, swamps, and grizzly bears. You had to find all those on your own.

Food procurement came next. Since the closest supermarket was one hundred miles away, we had to find our own. We could eat anything we could catch if we thought we could keep it down. They went through ten minutes of how to build snares, and told us how to fish. Just take your dry hook and drop it in the water. Let it settle to the bottom of the stream for a second. Pull the hook straight up, and if there were any trout in the stream, they would hit the hook. That was the craziest fishing technique I ever heard of, but I paid attention. That was the full extent of food procurement. Apparently they didn't think we would have time to hunt, and boy were they correct.

"O.K.," they said, "that concludes the school." "You have an hour to go find some food." "After that, we have to travel to the safe area." "It's over that mountain." "Bon appitit."

They left! Great! Joe and I looked at each other and then looked at our surroundings. We were standing in a little alpine valley. There were only a scattering of trees. The valley was level out in front of us and there was a small stream running down off the mountain. When I say small stream, I mean tiny. It was no more than thirteen and half inches wide and looked to be six inches deep. It wouldn't even be called a ditch at home. It looked like run-off coming down through the grass. From the stream, the ground seemed to rise gradually to a small mountain where trees began to grow in earnest. There were patches of snow all over the bare ground. It had been very cold earlier in the day but seemed to be about 32 degrees now. The sun was shining but was not adding warmth and the sky was a pale azure.

Joe looked at me and said, "Russ, how long has it been since we last ate?"

"I don't know." "I've lost track of time." "It's been two days at least."

He said, "How are we supposed to find anything?" "I can see for three miles in every direction and there is nothing."

I said, "The only thing I see is that stream over there."

He said, "What stream; "that little trickle of water?"

"You got any better idea?"

"No."

We walked despondently over to the little trickle of water and morosely looked down into it. You could see the bottom clear as day and there weren't any fish.

I said, "I know this is a waste of time, but I'm going to wet a hook."

All Joe could do was snort.

I unrolled my line and dropped the hook into the water, letting it settle to the bottom. I kneeled and began to slowly pull it straight up. Out of nowhere a trout came up and hit the hook. I could see him coming up, and my face was so close to the water I thought he was going to hit me in the eye; however, he hit the hook, and I pulled a nice trout out of the water.

You could have pushed Joe over with a feather. All you could see was blue eyes looking at the fish.

He said, "I'll build a fire." "I don't like mine raw." "Catch some more."

I said, "How are you planning to build a fire?"

He said, "I snuck some matches."

Joe went trotting off looking for sticks, and I dropped my hook back in the exact same spot. The results were the same. I caught another fair sized trout.

I began to fish in earnest then because I could have eaten a dozen trout, but no matter how hard I tried, I couldn't catch any more. By this time, Joe had a fire going and was roasting trout and two onions.

Joe and I sat down to a nice meal of hot trout and roasted onion. All the other guys were sitting around eating raw onion and looking at us with murder in their eyes. So far, Joe and I had made a pretty good team.

Chapter 26 – Getting Started

The friendlies showed up just as we were finishing up sucking the bones and warming our feet.   They looked a little surprised but didn't say anything.

They showed us how to make improvised backpacks out of parachute shroud line and how to tote the sleeping bags on our back. They instructed us to put the poncho on so that it covered the sleeping bags on our back. We would soon learn the significance of this.

Everybody lined out in a long line and the trek began. We went across the open meadow that looked flat, but it had a little tilt to it and was a little like walking on a treadmill with an awkward weight on your back.

By the time we made the tree line, I was huffing a little bit. When we hit the trees, we began to see what we were in for. The terrain got significantly steeper and the trees were growing at about two foot intervals, which wouldn't allow passage of shoulders and a backpack. You had to wiggle and shove your way past each and every tree trunk. I had been correct when I surmised that the temperature was about 32 degrees because the snow on the spruce branches was beginning to melt. As we shoved our way through the tight spaces between the trees, the boughs would jostle and water would rain down on us just like a winter shower. We got wet quick. In addition, the exertion level was extreme. You had to push the tree trunks apart and pull yourself uphill. Those trees would slap together behind you, and you had to make the same maneuver in order to move forward again. It was like swimming through trees.

The only thing that saved us was that it had been a little mountain. We finally reached the summit and went over to the other side. There was a thinned out space over there which was the safe zone. We began to prepare for the night.

We got a fire going and gathered up a pile of dry wood. While one person set-up the shelter, the other would dry sleeping bags. When the shelter was complete and the sleeping bags were dry, we began to dry our clothing by standing close to the fire.

As we dried out clothing, we had to build the fire higher because the temperature was dropping like a rock. If it kept this up, it would be in the low teens by nine o'clock.

We took our boots off, stepping on our sleeping bag to keep our feet dry. Off came the coat, which went on top of the sleeping bag. We then dived into the bags and closed off the top of the bag so that we were completely encapsulated in sleeping bag. We then waited for our body heat to warm the bag before we began stripping off naked. I piled all my clothes around my head to help stop drafts that come into the bag. If you got the drafts stopped and lay absolutely still, you would stay warm. If you wiggled so much as a toe, a stream of near zero air would rush into your sleeping bag. You had to be still.

It had been a long, long time since I had had sleep. I was exhausted. I could feel the sleeping bag getting warmer and warmer, and my body began to relax more and more. It was pitch black outside and the temperature kept dropping. Slowly and quietly the snow began to fall completely unknown to Joe and me. Our snores rattled the boughs of the spruce and fir trees. We were getting our first good night's sleep in three days. If I had been in a five star hotel, I wouldn't have slept any better.

Chapter 27 – The Chase Begins

It seemed that I had just closed my eyes when all this screaming and yelling commenced.

"Get up!" "Get up!" "We are being overrun." "We have to pull out!" "Now!"

I stuck my head out of my sleeping bag, and it was so cold that my breath got caught in my lungs. It was just daylight. I had slept twelve hours and it seemed like only minutes. I was more tired than I realized.

I quickly dressed inside my sleeping bag, and Joe and I rolled out at the same time almost knocking our tent down. We quickly rolled the sleeping bags and put them on our backs while ripping the ponchos apart and sliding them over everything. I looked at Joe and his teeth were chattering. I know I must look the same way.

A friendly appeared out of nowhere and handed me a map. He put his finger on a spot and said, "We are here."

Putting his finger on another spot, he said, "You have to get to this point before five p.m. otherwise you will be captured." "You must start right away."

Joe whipped out a compass and we got a general direction and faded into the woods. All this had taken less than three minutes from the time the screaming started.

Once hidden in a spot where we could observe our surroundings without being observed, we took the map out and actually plotted a course to follow and triangulated our present position.

In evasion, you never travel on trails or roads. You always select the roughest terrain. When traveling in the mountains, you always travel two thirds of the way up the face of the mountain. If someone attacks you from above, you can beat him down the mountain. If someone attacks from below, you can beat him to the top. If you think that is easy just go into the mountains sometime and pick a mountain. Climb two thirds of the way up and then travel along the face of the mountain where there are absolutely no trails. See how far you get and how much energy it takes.

That was exactly what Joe and I had to do. We could look at our map and see that the route lay right along the side of a mountain.

We started off at a good strong pace with Joe in the lead and me giving him terrain markers to aim for. We soon found that whoever broke trail would have to be alternated. The man that went first suffered most. When he brushed by trees, snow would pour off the braches down over his head and shoulders. The night before, we had had at least two or three inches of new snow. It was hanging on the tree branches in large clusters and fell heavily on the first person through.

Joe may have been born at night, but it wasn't last night. He soon tired of being pummeled by snow, and he wanted to navigate; so, we alternated the lead position for the next two hours.

When you have a straight line path to follow on a map, it is the shortest distance to get there, and if you are able to stay on it, you are more likely not to get lost or turned around.

However, there can be some daunting obstacles along a straight line. Sometimes you can go around them fairly easily and get right back on course. Sometimes the detour would be too long and take too much time. In those cases, you have to find a way to cross the obstacle.

Our first true test came in the form of a log jam on the side of a mountain. It was a monumental monster. It looked as big as the mountain itself and had openings that you could fall into and perhaps be killed. In addition, it was covered in snow, making it difficult to see the openings. The mountain to the left of the jam was too steep to climb and the area to the right was crisscrossed with huge, steep-sided gullies. There was no way to traverse either side, which left only straight ahead, and that was scary.

We decided to go one person at a time with the lead guy poking with a stick to find the surest footing. Up, up, up we went. Then we crawled across the top like two snow covered snakes. Finally down the other side, all the time looking into holes that seemed to have no bottom. Finally we made it to the other side of the jam, exhausted and sweating in spite of the cold.

Man was that tough. We decided to find a spot in the sun and triangulate our position to see how far we had traveled. It was about 9 a.m. and we had been traveling at a steady pace for four hours. We had eight hours left. Hopefully, we would be over half way there.

We triangulated our position and put a little mark on our map. We had only gone one third of the way, not one half. Some fast calculations told us we would have a twelve hour trek. This was no walk-in-the-park like I had hoped. This would be painful. All we could do was look at each other and shake our heads. Words weren't necessary. In addition, we were so drained of nutrition we didn't have energy to gripe.

From where we sat, the terrain did not look as bad as we had just traveled, but it covered a lot of footsteps. Thankfully, the temperature had begun to rise and it actually felt good outside.

The warmer temperatures brought a problem unique to itself. The snow began to melt off the trees and water began to rain down on us whether we touched trees or not. In addition the ground became slick and walking with a top-heavy back pack was difficult and tiring. We just walked for hours and hours changing leads ever so often to give each other a break. We would occasionally triangulate the map to find our position and look at our watches to confirm the pace. There was no time for taking breaks. We had to stay steady at it.

About four o'clock we saw the camp fire from the safe zone through the trees, and we knew we had made the first leg. We silently strode into camp and found a place to shelter. We made a fire right away and began drying everything out. We were really soaked. Steam was boiling off our clothes as we stood around the fire.

For the next hour, pairs of pilgrims silently strode into the safe zone until ten pair had arrived. All made the first leg and all were soaking wet and exhausted.

Chapter 28 – Exhaustion Sets In

Joe and I made our shelter, dried our clothes and climbed into bed hungry again. We slept like dead men again. The temperature dropped like a rock and snow silently fell all night.

When roused out the next morning, we had snow coverage, not snow patches. Snow was beginning to build on the ground, making walking more difficult. It was in that stage where it was beginning to build but was not deep enough for snowshoes.

We went through the same scenario of receiving a map and having to skulk out of camp the next morning. Again we had bright sunshine that contained little warmth, but would drip from the trees each afternoon. Again we had another arduous march across true wilderness. About every two hours, we would come to some obstacle that had to be overcome in quick time.

Fatigue derived from hunger and hard work is difficult to describe. After a while, you get past the driving hunger. You just feel empty. However, you can't get by the overlaying exhaustion that comes about from starvation. Each day you can tell that you are a little slower physically. You don't think well. You find that you have to concentrate on just putting one foot in front of the other, then dragging the first one forward again. Time begins to have no meaning. We had to constantly double-check our progress with the map and watch. We couldn't keep up with it otherwise. We didn't care if we got wet. We knew it was going to happen anyway. Pain from straining joints and tendons was a constant companion.

Somewhere in your brain there was a constant warning of "try not to get hurt." If you do, you won't survive.

Joe and I found that if we took the effort to talk to each other as we trudged along that would give our brains something pleasant to concentrate on rather than rehashing all the aches and pains. We had pretty much learned how to navigate in a wilderness and were pretty good at it. We had learned to avoid obstacles that we could avoid and traverse the ones that we could not avoid. It was walk all day and fall into a hunger induced fatigue sleep each night. It was cold, it was wet, it was miserable, and it went on like this for four days.

Chapter 29 – Blizzard

The morning of the fifth day dawned, extremely cold, but not clear. At least water wouldn't drip on us today. There was no way the temperature would rise above freezing with the sun not shining. The atmosphere had a funny feel to it. It was a little like it feels at home just before it snows only this had a cutting, dangerous feel to it.

Joe and I got our map and, as we had done for the past four days, we sat down on a rock and studied it. Sure seemed like they had saved the worst for last. Just from studying the map, it looked like we were going into some mean country. The trail went through areas where the elevation lines were very close together on both sides of the trail. That meant steep walled canyons both left and right. If we encountered deadfalls and other obstacles, it was going to sap all our strength to get through.

Joe just looked at me. There was no need for words. The map could have had a loud speaker attached to it and wouldn't have been any clearer. This was going to be hell's last gasp.

Joe said, "This is the last day." "If we make it on time, it's over." "I can do it."

I said, "I'm sure not spending the night in the woods while you graduate." "I can do it too."

The map wasn't wrong. This was a gut buster. There were blow downs, steep gullies, sheer mountain slopes, dense trees, awful rock formations to scramble over, deep snow from the days before, tons of snow falling off branches, slippery trails, and the blizzard.

The day started out cold and overcast with a bad feel. The feel didn't improve as we struggled along. It began with just a few flakes that were nearly as big as my hand. We were about half way down the trail when that started.

We doubled our effort. We were southern boys and, down south, when a snow starts off with a few, big flakes, it's going to be scary. The flakes started to come down faster with the size of the flakes decreasing which is another bad sign.

We were moving along almost at a dog trot now. We were blowing like long distance runners struggling to draw in oxygen. Great geysers of steam poured forward in front of us from each breath. Ice hung down three inches long off our coyote fur parkas.

Then the wind began, slowly at first, just moving the tree limbs above our heads. The snow that had been accumulating all week on the limbs poured off on us like a giant avalanche. Even though it wasn't snowing that hard yet, the tree snow made it difficult to see and we began having trouble finding our check points. We simply couldn't see.

The tree snow lasted for an hour or so before all the snow had been stripped from the tree limbs. We could see again and quickly triangulated our position. Surprisingly, we were fairly close to the safe camp, but the remaining terrain was horrible, very steep and sheer with deep gullies. We had to be careful. We didn't want to get close and then get hurt because we were hurrying.

We slowed down and began a steady swinging walk. That was when it really began to snow. It was snowing so hard we could barely make out our check points. The chances of getting hopelessly lost were increasing. We had to be even more careful.

The wind really began to blow. The snow was no longer coming straight down, but had a considerable sideways slant to it, plus the temperature dropped. It got really cold.

I told Joe to stop. We had to figure something out. I figured we were no more than two miles from the camp, but it may as well have been two million miles. It was snowing too hard to navigate anymore. You couldn't see fifty feet and everything looked the same.

We were standing in a very narrow valley between two steep slopes. I could see it on the map, but that didn't do us any good because I couldn't see the actual landmarks surrounding us. I began to look at the map hoping to see some shelter close by. Joe was looking over my shoulder and we were both getting a little antsy.

Then I saw something on the map. I showed it to Joe. Above us on our left side, about 100 feet up was a small flat ridge, and, according to the map, it wound around the mountain and ended-up right at the camp site. Joe looked it over closely and came to the same conclusion I had reached. If we could reach that ridge, we wouldn't have to be able to see to navigate. We could just follow the ridge and walk into camp. We still had a chance, but when we looked at the face of the mountain we had a sinking feeling. It was almost straight up, not quite, but almost. It would be like climbing an artificial rock wall, although not quite so steep.

Joe said, "Come on, Russ." "Let's do it," and he began to climb. I was right beside him, and I am not a mountain climber. I'm afraid of heights, but this did have a slight slope so it wasn't vertical. This helped some, but it didn't alleviate the sheer effort it took to climb the face of the cliff.

Slowly we inched upward, one hand hold at a time. It was pull up, look for a hand hold, look for a foot hold, pull up, and start over. Finally my eyes were above the ridge, then my chest, and I rolled onto my belly and lay face down in the snow. To my right, Joe was lying on his belly and looking me in the eyes. We were both almost too exhausted to pick our heads up out of the snow.

Joe said something prophetic. He said, "I can crawl to camp from here."

I said, "I agree." "But it will be better to walk into camp." "Get up and let's ride."

We stumbled and staggered to our feet. We were almost too tired to stand. We had to weave for a second before we could lean in the proper direction.

The ridge was about ten feet wide and was as flat as a highway. I couldn't believe our good luck and Joe and I were staggering along discussing our good luck. I walked a few steps and I said, "Joe, I can almost smell the smoke from the camp fire." "We can't be more than a mile away."

I expected some answer, but got none. I looked to my right and Joe was gone. I turned around and around trying to locate him in the blowing snow, but he wasn't there. I looked down to the snow and only saw one set of footprints, mine. I had been walking next to the cliff face and Joe had been walking along the edge of the ridge. I kept saying to myself, "he just fell down." "I'll see him in a second."

What I saw was where his footprints trailed off the side of the ridge. He had gotten dizzy and fallen down the mountain!

I ran to where he had gone over, ripping off my backpack. I dropped to my knees and looked over the edge. I could barely see him, far below, lying on his back. His shape was somewhat blurry, but I could clearly see his blue eyes. They must have been as big as saucers.

I yelled down, "Joe, are you alright?"

"No."

"Well, what's wrong with you?"

"I hurt my right leg." "I can move it, but I can't get up."

"Hang on, I'm coming down."

I went over the edge, feet-first, and began the long, slow climb down the sheer face. I had to be careful. If I got hurt too, it was lights out for both of us. It was so cold that my hands began to go numb and the wind was rushing along the cliff face at a steady velocity. It made it difficult to put my feet squarely on a safe step.

I made it and got beside him. Nothing was broken, but he looked like he had been run over by a Mac Truck. I scrounged around and found him a tree limb that made a pretty good crutch. I had to strip off his backpack before he could stand. He looked like a walrus with big ice tusks hanging down. The very first thing he did was start complaining about his weenie being cold. Against my better judgment, I did an inspection and found that he had ripped his trousers open right in front, and yes, I bet his weenie was cold.

He said, "You'll have to warm that up."

"No hope for that." "You are going to get frostbite." "Stuff some moss down in there."

He said, "Well, find some and stuff it in my pants." "My weenie is going to fall off."

I went mumbling into the forest and came back with a big handful. Problem was, it was crusted up with snow and ice, but I figured it was better than the north wind. Having no doubt that he was cold, I packed his weenie, ice and all. He really howled then, but I didn't pay him any attention. All my focus was how was I to get him up that cliff face? I was already so tired that I could hardly stand before I climbed down the thing, and so was Joe. Now he couldn't walk. We weren't dead yet, but we were in a big, big mess.

I shouldered his backpack and held onto his good side. With his crutch on one side and me on the other we staggered to the cliff face and leaned against it. Again, we just looked at each other. His was the, "if we don't do it this time, we are both dead" look. I was getting tired of his looks. They just seemed to work into bigger and bigger problems.

I don't know how Joe did it, but he began to climb. I could hear him sobbing in pain and sometimes I had to catch him on his weak side to keep him from falling. I was coming up the cliff with me, his backpack, and half of Joe. My arms began to tremble, my hands had been numb for a long time, and my feet and legs felt like they were made of lead, but still Joe climbed.

Above the howling wind I could hear another sound. It sounded like Patsy barking at me from heaven. She seemed to be saying, "Come on." "This is what I trained you for." "If you can't find a foothold, don't give up." "Search for another." "Work from daylight to dark." "Fight like a Ninja." "This isn't playtime, this is what I trained you for."

Slowly we inched upward, more slowly than the first time. If I began to run out of gas and couldn't push anymore, Joe seemed to sense it and would redouble his efforts. We went from one hand hold to the next. I couldn't look up to get a position on the ridge. It was too much strain. I just had to trust that we would make it sometime.

My left hand felt the ridge! Joe said, "I feel the ridge." I got my shoulder under him and gave him a stable platform so he could crawl up. I was too exhausted to help.

He went over onto the ridge and reached back over and helped me over. Again we lay in the snow, face to face.

Joe said, "Man, I can't even crawl now."

I said, "Between the two of us, I think we can walk."

Chapter 31 – Last Legs

I got up and dragged his heavy butt over to the cliff face so he couldn't fall off again. I put on my backpack and carried his backpack in my right hand. After much grunting on his part and more complaints about his weenie, I got him on his feet, and we began a slow traverse of the ridge toward camp.

In all this travail I had blocked out the weather, but it was still there, snowing like crazy with howling wind and almost dark at 4 p.m. It didn't matter. We could feel the cliff face. All we had to do was slide along it, and that was exactly what we did.

Up ahead we saw the fire. It was huge. I guess they were trying to make it into a beacon for us. Joe and I came staggering into camp, more dead than alive. One of the Instructors saw us and came running to help me with Joe.

I told him what had happened and what he told me was bone chilling. The weather was so bad that transportation couldn't get to us. We would have to spend the night in this hell. Also we had to do with what we had. There were no Medics as well. This was true survival conditions.

We dragged Joe as close to the big fire as possible. We were both soaking wet. The fall through the snow plus all the exertion had produced a ton of sweat and it was freezing on us, especially Joe. All he could do was huddle on the ground and shiver from the cold.

I built a shelter as fast as I could build it and got Joe out of the wind and snow, but it was plenty cold, even with a fire.

I got Joe's sleeping bags and dried them. That took two hours at least. I put his bags together and put them in the shelter.

The Instructor came around with food, a cup of hot broth and a Graham cracker. I've never tasted anything that tasted better. That was the first food in nearly a week.

I stripped Joe butt naked and shoved him in the warm sleeping bags. I could see the sleeping bag bouncing up and down from him shivering.

I dried his clothes, one piece at a time, and shoved each hot piece of clothing into his sleeping bag with him. By midnight, I had his stuff dry, and he was snoring loud enough to raise the dead. At least he was alright.

Now I began on my sleeping bag and clothes. I was done with the bags by 2 a.m. and my clothes were dry by 3 a.m. I was snoring just like Joe by 3:01 a.m.

Chapter 32 – Hell Finally Ends

We were roused out of our sleeping bags at 5 a.m. , and we were informed that transportation had arrived. It was on a dirt road that could be seen at the base of the mountain, down a fairly steep slope. The busses were about a quarter mile away. We were informed that school wasn't over. We had to make it to the buses on our own or we would fail and have to do the whole thing over. They weren't kidding either. We later found out that five pairs had spent the night in that blizzard, and some had almost died. They all had to take the course over, prison camp and all.

I didn't think I would ever get Joe on his feet. He was one big black and blue bruise, and, of course, he was complaining bitterly about his weenie. He wouldn't let me stuff it with icy moss again. I guess real men can stand thirty minutes at zero degrees.

We began to make our way down the slope. The trees were spaced about ten yards apart, so we could get started and catch ourselves on the next tree. We were too weak to walk down the hill in normal fashion.

As I leaned on one of the trees for support, I remember looking back over my shoulder up the hill. There were guys crawling on their hands and knees, there were guys scooting along on their butts, and others had just lay down and given up. A colonel was walking among them yelling at the top of his lungs, "Get up!" "You will die if you lay here." "Move." "Move."

Joe and I just kept stumbling from tree to tree and finally reached the bus sitting on the road. We both slammed into the side of it with our faces lying against it, looking each other in the eye one last time.

I remember Joe saying, "Damn Russ, we made it!"

We slid along the bus to the door and crawled up the steps to a seat. I remember sitting in the seat next to Joe and then everything went blank.

The bus traveled back to Fairchild, we got off, gathered our diplomas, packed, and I traveled to Seattle and caught a flight to Denver. From Denver, I flew into Charleston, S.C. and took a cab to my mother-in-law's house. I remember none of it. My mind totally wiped that slate clean. This is called dissociative amnesia. The shrinks say that it is linked to overwhelming stress, which might be the result of traumatic events such as war, abuse, accidents, or disaster. As I write this, I wonder if I fall into any one of these or if I fall into all of them at one time? I would be a psychiatric nightmare.

My memory picks back up as I walk into the kitchen. I've lost thirty pounds, I'm bruised and battered, and my eyes are sunk back in my head. This won't be the last time that I do this to my wife.

She said, "What happened to you?"

"School."

She said, "You just went to a little course on survival."

"This was Military School, not Kindergarten like you are used to."

I said, "I'm going to bed and I plan to sleep for a week if I don't starve to death before I wake up."

This all occurred in 1970. I didn't see Joe King again for 46 years until I met him at a Pilot's reunion in Charleston.

As usual, I was thrilled to see him, and, as usual, he looked at me as if he were afraid the devil would jump out from behind me. I had been thinking about writing about this for about a year, and, now, I had a chance to question Joe about his memories and compare them with mine.

I said, "Joe, do you remember the time we were in survival training, and you fell down that mountain?"

"No, I don't remember that."

"Don't you remember the hard time we had tracking through the woods?"

"No." "I don't remember any of that and you can't make me believe it really happened."

I was totally flabbergasted. I was actually distraught and went several months considering just giving up on the idea of writing this story. Only two people in the world know what happened. Nobody is going to believe it, and now Joe doesn't remember or believe it. I was actually depressed. Then I remembered something Joe told me that changed my mind.

He said, "I did go to a civilian doctor when I got back home." "I took my shoe off and put my foot on the examination table, and I said, "Doc, are those two middle toes supposed to be black like that?"

Well, that did it. I couldn't let it rest. I realized that I could say anything I wanted. Nobody could confirm it, not even Joe, but nobody could deny it either. So, with that, I put the ball squarely in your court. Really, how true is this story?

When I talked to Joe, he had me so bumfuzzled that I forgot to ask him the most important question of all.

Joe, what did the doctor say when you plopped your weenie across the examination table?

Made in the USA
Monee, IL
16 May 2022

96530466R00075